100

THINGS TO DO ON
ROUTE 66
BEFORE YOU
DIE

100
THINGS TO DO ON
ROUTE 66
BEFORE YOU
DIE

JIM HINCKLEY

REEDY PRESS

Library of Congress Control Number: 2017934671

ISBN: 9781681061023

Design by Jill Halpin

Printed in the United States of America
17 18 19 20 21   5 4 3 2 1

Please note that websites, phone numbers, addresses, and company names are subject to change or cancellation. We did our best to relay the most accurate information available, but due to circumstances beyond our control, please do not hold us liable for misinformation. When exploring new destinations, please do your homework before you go.

DEDICATION

To my dearest friend, fellow traveler, and moral officer, thank you for thirty-five years of companionship on the road less traveled. To the international Route 66 community, thank you for transforming this storied old highway into America's longest attraction.

• •

CONTENTS

Great Eats, the Ultimate Route 66 Time Capsule—Route 66 Restaurants

● ●

Neon Nights and Rooms with a View

● ●

Memory-Making Photo Stops

Must-See Attractions

PREFACE

Route 66, or the "Mother Road" as John Steinbeck referred to it in *The Grapes of Wrath*, was certified on November 11, 1926. In 1927, a brilliant marketing campaign launched by the U.S. Highway 66 Association labeled it the "Main Street of America." On June 27, 1985, the American Association of State Highway and Transportation Officials removed it from the roster of federal highways. It was the end of an era.

Surprisingly, the highway that does not officially exist is more popular than at any time in its history. There are companies operating in at least five countries that specialize in Route 66 tours. There are active Route 66 associations in Europe, Australia, Japan, and South America, and in the summer of 2016, the Route 66 Association of Germany hosted the first European Route 66 festival.

Route 66 in the twenty-first century is no mere highway. It is the stuff of dreams—a magical place where the past, the present, and even the future blend seamlessly. It is a string of living time capsules, a neon-lit wonderland filled with quirky museums, stunning landscapes, fascinating restaurants, historic sites, landmarks, and small towns that seem lifted from Norman Rockwell prints.

It is the ultimate American road trip. It is the ultimate bucket list, and here are 100 things you need to see on Route 66 before you die.

ACKNOWLEDGMENTS

Where do I begin? First, there is my dearest friend, an amazing woman who has been my traveling companion on Route 66 and the road less traveled for more than three decades. Her gentle encouragement and steadfast support ensured that this project made the transition from idea to book.

It is the people who travel Route 66, the people who keep the memories alive and preserve the road's dusty history, and the people who keep the neon shining bright and the coffee warm that give this amazing old road its magic, its vitality. Thank you.

Then there is our Route 66 family, those amazing and generous people who made suggestions and shared memories, as well as their passion, for this storied old road. I am appreciative of your contributions, camaraderie, and friendship.

● ●

Antares
Point

RANCHERO

Home Of
GIGANTICUS HEADICUS

KOZY
CORNER
RV

PARK

Gifts

BARBED WIRE, ELECTRIC CARS, AND COWBOYS– ROUTE 66 MUSEUMS

ABRAHAM LINCOLN PRESIDENTIAL LIBRARY AND MUSEUM

State-of-the-art, full-immersion exhibits including a holographic movie, special effects theaters, and displays of original artifacts make this one of the premier experience museums in the nation. Through extensive use of advanced entertainment technology, the visitor can experience the life and times of Abraham Lincoln by stepping into his world. The museum has three primary sections: Abraham Lincoln before his election as president, the Abraham Lincoln presidency, and Illinois history in the nineteenth century.

Two hours would be wholly inadequate to experience this stunning museum in its entirety. The 200,000-square-foot complex includes an archive and library, the largest repository of original materials in the world pertaining to the sixteenth president, and consistently receives favorable reviews on TripAdvisor and Yelp. Some exhibits, however, are not suitable for younger children because of their graphic and realistic nature.

112 N. 6th St., Springfield, IL 62701

www.alplm.org

TIP

A few blocks away, at 413 South 8th Street, the National Park Service preserves the home of Abraham Lincoln and provides tours. The home is the centerpiece of the Lincoln Neighborhood, with restored or recreated homes and properties preserved as they were in 1860 before Lincoln's election as president.

CAHOKIA MOUNDS STATE HISTORIC SITE

The 2,200-acre park is but a fragment of what was once the largest city north of Mexico. Conservative estimates are that in AD 1250 Cahokia was a larger and possibly more modern city than London. Preserved in the park today are seventy of the eighty remaining mounds, including Monks Mound, which towers to one hundred feet in height with a fourteen-acre base. Considered one of the largest and most complex pre-Columbian archaeological sites in the United States, Cahokia is a national historic landmark. It's also one of only twenty-three designated UNESCO World Heritage Sites in the United States.

Before exploring the site, visitors should first stop at the interpretive center to learn more about the highly complex society that built a city along the Mississippi River more than a thousand years ago. The center also has maps of the various sites located throughout the grounds, as well as audio tour information.

30 Ramey St., Collinsville, IL 62234

www.cahokiamounds.org

VACUUM CLEANER MUSEUM AND FACTORY OUTLET STORE

Get sucked into history at the vacuum cleaner museum in St. James, Missouri. Perhaps the most amazing thing about this museum is that it is actually interesting and fascinating!

Located in a factory outlet store, this free museum does more than chronicle every aspect of vacuum cleaner development since 1900. The story of door-to-door sales, the rise of consumer finance that transformed America, and the evolution of industrial production in the twentieth century is told through the history of the vacuum cleaner.

The displays, arranged by decade in settings that mimic the living room in each era, include vintage televisions, hi-fi stereos, and radios, as well as vacuum cleaner promotional materials and original packaging. This allows for the display of the vacuum cleaners in a period-correct, time-capsule setting.

The curator of the collection is Tom Gasko, a fellow whose passion for the vacuum cleaner, its history, and its role in the evolution of American society is infectious. He ensures that a visit to the museum will be entertaining, educational, and surprisingly fun.

3 Industrial Dr., St. James, MO 65559

www.vacuummuseum.com

J.M. DAVIS ARMS AND HISTORICAL MUSEUM

With more than twenty thousand firearms and firearm-related items ranging from historic cannons and artillery pieces to guns that once belonged to celebrities and outlaws, this is *the* ultimate firearm museum. Here you will find collections that trace the evolution of Colt and Winchester, as well as the Czechoslovakian small-arms industry. There are even guns designed specifically for the whaling industry. Guns, however, are but the tip of the iceberg at this fascinating museum.

Also on display are more than one thousand historic military German beer steins, statuary by John Rogers, and a staggering collection of ornate nineteenth-century music boxes, World War I recruitment posters (American as well as German), swords, knives, Native American artifacts, and an array of historic taxidermy. Additionally, if you're interested in the macabre, there's a display of hoods and nooses used in famous executions.

330 N. J.M. Davis Blvd., Claremore, OK 74017

www.thegunmuseum.com

TIP

A few blocks from the J.M. Davis Arms and Historical Museum is the Will Rogers Memorial Museum and Birthplace Ranch at 1720 West Will Rogers Boulevard. Preserved at the expansive complex that consists of historic buildings, landscaped grounds, and monuments is an array of Will Rogers displays and artifacts, including original recordings.

FOREST PARK

Established on June 24, 1876, Forest Park underwent extensive expansion and construction in preparation for the 1904 World's Fair, which was held in the park. Today the park, which is larger than Central Park in New York City, is home to the Missouri History Museum, the Saint Louis Art Museum, a horticultural facility, a sculpture park, the Saint Louis Science Center, the Muny, and the Saint Louis Zoo. The Saint Louis Art Museum's main building dates to the World's Fair. In 1913, a monument to Thomas Jefferson was constructed, and today this building houses the Missouri History Museum.

The Saint Louis Zoo opened in 1910, and in its centennial year it attracted 2.9 million visitors. Over the course of the past decade, the zoo and park have undergone dramatic restoration and transformation. As an example, the introduction of prairie and wetlands areas has created natural habitats for a variety of birds and native wildlife.

5595 Grand Dr., St. Louis, MO 63112

GALENA MINING AND HISTORICAL MUSEUM

A restored Missouri-Texas-Kansas Railroad depot that was relocated to the site and a larger building at the rear of the facility house most exhibits and displays. As Galena was once a major lead and zinc mining center, extensive mineral displays are a focal point. However, the exhibits are quite diverse and include the oil paintings of local artist Carol Bliss-Riley, which were once displayed at the Smithsonian Institution. Historic photographs and detailed dioramas chronicle the area's rich and colorful history.

Other relics are displayed on the expansive grounds. These include large, century-old machines used in the mines and a surprising array of military equipment ranging from a Vietnam-era helicopter to a World War II anti-aircraft gun emplacement. Railroad equipment, including a caboose, is also on display.

BAXTER SPRINGS HERITAGE MUSEUM

Since Baxter Springs was once at the center of the richest lead and zinc mining district in the world and was the site of a pivotal Civil War battle, the array of fascinating exhibits is not surprising. What is surprising, though, is the number and diversity of those exhibits housed in a 20,000-square-foot facility without presenting the appearance that the museum is an overcrowded attic. Mining exhibits and displays that provide insight into the African American experience, as well as into the city's vital importance in World War I and World War II, are but a sample of the fascinating collections on display in this amazing small-town museum.

Did you know that Mickey Mantle kicked off his professional career with the Baxter Springs Whiz Kids? Did you know that the Osage Indians believed the mineral springs found here had healing properties, or that the city hosted Grand Army of the Republic reunions for several years after the Civil War?

740 East Ave., Baxter Springs, KS 66713

www.baxterspringsmuseum.org

TIP

While at the museum, pick up a map for the self-guided driving tour to the twelve kiosks that mark the course of the Battle of Baxter Springs during the Civil War. The final stop on the tour is at the National Cemetery, dedicated to those who lost their lives during this confrontation between Union and Confederate forces.

NATIONAL COWBOY & WESTERN HERITAGE MUSEUM

This is the ultimate stop for anyone with an interest in the history, culture, allure, legend, and romance of the American West. Established in 1955, the museum houses one of the world's largest collections of Western art and artifacts and sponsors an array of educational programs. Since opening, more than ten million visitors from around the world have signed the guest book.

On display is a renowned collection of work by artists such as Frederick Remington, Charles Russell, and James Earl Fraser. In the exhibition wing, the visitor can explore a Western frontier town or interactive galleries dedicated to the American cowboy, historic firearms, the military on the Western frontier, Native American culture, medicine shows, and performers. For visitors with families, landscaped grounds flank the Children's Cowboy Corral.

1700 NE 63rd St., Oklahoma City, OK 73111

www.nationalcowboymuseum.org

U.S. CAVALRY MUSEUM AND RESEARCH LIBRARY

Opened in April 2015 and housed in the former officers' duplex, the Cavalry Museum preserves a vast and diverse collection of artifacts, some of which date back to the Revolutionary War. This, however, is just one of several points of interest at this historic fort established in 1874.

The complex has a colorful and diverse history. The legendary buffalo soldiers were stationed here during the Indian Wars, and in 1908 the facility served as the Army Quartermaster Remount Station, a facility for the training of horses and pack mules. Surprisingly, the fort served as a remount station until 1948.

Found in the cemetery and the chapel are links to another fascinating chapter in the fort's history. During World War II, German and Italian POWs captured in battles with General Rommel's Afrika Korps were interred here, and in 1944 they built the chapel. At the west end of the post cemetery are the graves of seventy POWs. Every November, a German-American Heritage Day is held at the fort.

Exit 119 East off I-40 to Rte. 66, El Reno, OK 73036

www.fortreno.org

NEW MEXICO HISTORY MUSEUM

This museum is a campus that includes the Palace Press, the Fray Angélico Chávez History Library and Photo Archives, and the Palace of the Governors. Permanent, temporary, and special exhibits chronicle the history of New Mexico from its indigenous people and their culture to the Spanish colonial period, Mexican era, and American acquisition and development that includes the Santa Fe Trail and Route 66.

The Palace of the Governors and adjoining New Mexico History Museum house the main museum. Built upon the ruins of a Native American village in the early seventeenth century, this is the oldest continuously operated public building in the United States.

As an interesting historical footnote, territorial governor Lew Wallace wrote the final chapters of *Ben Hur: A Tale of the Christ* at the Palace of the Governors.

105 W. Palace Ave., Santa Fe, NM 87501

www.nmhistorymuseum.org

There are three opportunities to experience seventeenth and eighteenth century Spanish colonial history along Route 66. One of these is in Santa Fe, New Mexico. The survey for the historic plaza occurred in 1608. The Palace of the Governors, now a museum, was built in 1609 and is the oldest government building in the United States. A few blocks away is the San Miguel Mission, the oldest continuously operating church in the United States. Dating to 1610, portions of a twelfth-century pueblo were utilized in its construction.

MESALANDS DINOSAUR MUSEUM AND NATURAL HISTORY LABORATORY

With 10,000 square feet of exhibit space, displays are surprisingly expansive, ranging from tiny casts of prehistoric footprints to a forty-foot Torvosaurus skeleton. Utilizing the Mesalands Community College foundry, staff and students created skeletons and fossils replicated in bronze, which are on exhibit. A children's museum that includes ample opportunity for tactile interaction makes this a very family-friendly stop. Recently, the collection of Eocene-era leaves, fish, and insect fossils donated by the family of Howard Shanks, an eminent paleontologist and mineralogist, added to the museum's diversity.

In addition to the museum, an immersion into the world of the paleontologist is available through field classes offered by the college or customized digs arranged for groups. An extensive museum gift shop offering books, mineral samples, games, teaching aids, gift items, and souvenirs rounds out the complex.

222 E. Laughlin Ave., Tucumcari, NM 88401

www.mesalands.edu

LOS ANGELES POLICE MUSEUM

Built in 1926, the Highland Park police station served its original purpose until it closed in 1983. The station figured prominently in numerous famous cases. Detective Robert Grogan centered his investigation into the Hillside Strangler from this location, and in 1973 the Symbionese Liberation Army, made famous with the kidnapping of heiress Patty Hearst, planted a bomb at the station.

In addition to displays and exhibits pertaining to these cases, the museum, which opened in September 2001, preserves and chronicles the history of the Los Angeles Police Department since its establishment in 1869. Original jail cells, historic photographs, a vintage paddy wagon, uniforms, badges, squad cars, and even bullet-riddled vehicles from crime scenes are but a few of the things ensuring that a visit to this museum will be memorable.

6045 York Blvd. (Highland Park), Los Angeles, CA 90042

www.laphs.org

MOJAVE DESERT HERITAGE AND CULTURAL ASSOCIATION

Goffs, California, which was bypassed because of Route 66 realignment in 1931, is less than the proverbial wide spot in the road. Even the critically acclaimed museum housed in a renovated 1914 schoolhouse—the focal point for acres of diverse exhibits that range from vintage trucks and an operational ten-stamp mill to mineral displays and World War II items—has an Essex, California, mailing address. The museum is a surprising discovery in its remote location in the Mojave Desert.

The prehistory of the area, the Mojave Road (a mid-nineteenth-century road pivotal to the development of Southern California), railroading, mining, ranching, and even World War II are all part of the Goffs story preserved at this museum.

I suggest that you plan your visit for fall, winter, or early spring. Summer temperatures in this part of the desert often exceed 120 degrees.

37198 Lanfair Rd., Essex, CA 92332

www.mdhca.org

Ensuring that your Route 66 adventure is memorable and enjoyable begins with choosing a season for the trip. The months of summer are the most popular. However, from the Colorado River Valley to Barstow, Route 66 crosses the Mojave Desert and daytime temperatures often soar higher than 120 degrees during that period. Snowstorms are possible around Flagstaff, Arizona, as late as April. My preference is May through early June, or mid-September through October. In general, temperatures are milder, popular attractions are less crowded, several small-town festivals take place during spring and fall, and the fall colors enhance a drive through the Ozark Mountains. Additionally, desert temperatures are relatively mild.

BARSTOW ROUTE 66 MOTHER ROAD MUSEUM

This museum, as well as the adjoining railroad museum, are housed in the stunning Casa del Desierto, an architecturally significant Harvey House railroad hotel and depot built in 1911. The museum tells the history of Route 66 and its predecessor, the National Old Trails Highway, in the Mojave Desert, as well as their impact on Barstow. The gift shop, which includes a large bookstore, mirrors the museum with a large variety of books about Route 66 and the history of the desert, including the sprawling Marine Corps base established during World War II.

Exhibits that range from automobiles to photographs provide the visitor with a microcosmic view of the evolution of American society in the twentieth century as seen from the perspective of a small desert community. As with Route 66, though, what makes this museum stand out is the volunteer staff that is knowledgeable and passionate.

681 N. 1st Ave., Barstow, CA 92311

www.route66museum.org

At the 2014 Route 66 International Festival in Kingman, Arizona, an emphasis was placed on Route 66 being the crossroads of the past and future. There are now electric vehicle charging facilities all along the Route corridor, including Tesla-specific charging stations. If you're planning a Route 66 adventure in an electric vehicle, I suggest using the free Plug Share website.

https://www.plugshare.com/

DEVIL'S ROPE AND ROUTE 66 MUSEUM

Did you know that there are more than 450 patents for barbed wire? Did you know that there are more than two thousand variations of barbed wire?

Housed in a former brassiere factory, this museum is surprisingly interesting. Among the exhibits are hundreds of different types of barbed wire displayed against backdrops of historic documents, photos, vintage advertisements and catalogs, patent models, wire tools, and an array of memorabilia. The museum also includes sculptures created from barbed wire, exhibits that tell the story of Route 66 in Texas, and displays that tell the fascinating story of McLean, the last town in Texas on Route 66 bypassed by the interstate highway.

First impressions of the museum and the town itself are deceptive. This town was once known as the "uplift capital of Texas," and during World War II there was a POW camp east of town. There's also a direct connection with the sinking of the *Titanic* (the story is told at the museum).

100 Kingsley St., McLean, TX 79057

www.barbwiremuseum.com

NATIONAL ROUTE 66 MUSEUM

The National Route 66 Museum is part of the Old Town Museum Complex that also includes the Farm & Ranch Museum, the Transportation Museum, and the Blacksmith Museum. It's quite easy to spend a very full afternoon exploring all the exhibits, some of which are interactive.

One of the most fascinating displays in the National Route 66 Museum is a 1955 Cadillac convertible linked to a film and screen that allows the visitor to "drive" along U.S. 66 in Oklahoma. A similar exhibit provides an opportunity to experience a drive-in movie from the comfort of a Chevrolet Impala. Other displays and exhibits at the museum complex include a windmill collection and a historic cowboy and rodeo display donated by Beutler Brothers Rodeo Stock Producers, as well as Native American arts and crafts, vintage tractors, and a complete late-nineteenth-century doctor's office.

2717 W. 3rd St., Elk City, OK 73644

www.visitelkcity.com

ROUTE 66 ELECTRIC VEHICLE MUSEUM

In the summer of 2014, Kingman, Arizona, served as the host city for the annual International Route 66 Festival. The theme for that event was Kingman: Crossroads of the Past & Future. In a partnership with the Historic Electric Vehicle Foundation and the Kingman Tourism Department, the Route 66 Electric Vehicle Museum debuted at this event. Fittingly, the Powerhouse Visitor Center, a former electrical plant built in 1908 that is also the oldest reinforced concrete structure in Arizona, houses the collection of unique automobiles.

Vehicles on display at the museum range from the speed-record-setting *Buckeye Bullet* to a 1905 package truck, a very rare 1959 Henney Kilowatt, electric motorcycles, and microcars. Customized golf carts that once belonged to Willie Nelson and Waylon Jennings are also on display.

120 W. Andy Devine Ave., Kingman, AZ 86401

www.gokingman.com

When visiting the Route 66
Museum, don't miss . . .

The Powerhouse Visitor Center houses the
Arizona Visitors Center and the gift shop for the
Historic Route 66 Association of Arizona. On the
second floor is the critically acclaimed Arizona
Route 66 Museum and Main Street America,
a multimedia display created and donated by
Kingman native Bob Boze Bell, the publisher
of *True West* magazine, that provides a window
into the Kingman of the 1950s.

Opposite the Powerhouse, in Locomotive Park,
is a massive 1920s-era Baldwin steam-powered,
"mountain type" locomotive and caboose. At
the west end of the park, the Mohave Museum
of History & Arts has a wide array of exhibits
chronicling the history of Mohave County and
a room dedicated to Andy Devine, the character
actor and namesake for Andy Devine Avenue.
While you're in town, consider spending some
time seeking out unique photo ops. The Route
66 Association of Kingman has been working in
partnership with business owners to transform
blank walls into artistic masterpieces and to
relight the night with refurbished neon signage.
Just east of town are the former Kingman Army
Airfield, now the Kingman Airport & Industrial
Park, and Giganticus Headicus, a sculpture with
stunning landscapes as a backdrop.

NEW MEXICO MINING MUSEUM

The highlight of this museum is an opportunity to experience the life of a uranium miner through a well-crafted exhibit that presents the illusion of descending deep underground even though the "mine" is in the cellar. The self-guided tour allows visitors to immerse themselves in a mid-century mining experience. The museum also includes exhibits of historic Native American crafts, minerals, displays that chronicle the area's rich mining history, and photos from the era of Route 66. Mining equipment and related exhibits are displayed on the park-like grounds.

The museum, located in the Chamber of Commerce building, is free. A nominal fee, however, is charged for the mine tour, and although it's self-guided, retired miners will occasionally provide information that is more detailed.

100 Iron Gate Ave., Grants, NM 87020

www.grants.org

We enjoy driving to Springerville from Grants, New Mexico, on State Highway 53. You can also drive this as a scenic loop from Grants to Gallup that negates the need to drive on I-40. As a bonus, there are some fascinating attractions. El Malpais National Monument is a scenic wonderland of ancient lava flows, cinder cones, wind-carved sandstone bluffs, and lava tubes. Bandera Crater is quite scenic but it's the ice caves that really make this place special. El Morro National Monument with a towering sandstone monolith as the centerpiece is a natural wonder. However, it's the lengthy history of the site that makes it a special attraction. Above the monolith are the ruins of a one-thousand-year-old Native American village. At the base is a natural artesian well that has served as an oasis for travelers for centuries. Carved in the soft stone are petroglyphs and the names of famous explores such as Lt. Edward Fitzgerald Beale, Kit Carson, and Don Juan de Onate, a sixteenth-century Spanish explorer. The historic Zuni Pueblo is also located on this highway just south of Gallup. Europeans first visited the pueblo in 1539 in their search for the fabled seven cities of gold. Archaeological studies indicate that the Zuni people have farmed in the area for at least three thousand years. The pueblo dates to the fourteenth century.

GREAT EATS, THE ULTIMATE ROUTE 66 TIME CAPSULE– ROUTE 66 RESTAURANTS

PALMS GRILL CAFÉ

Diminutive Atlanta, Illinois, seems an unlikely destination for thousands of international travelers. Subtle advertising murals on nineteenth-century brick walls, the clock tower that casts long shadows in the late afternoon, and a unique arcade museum are not enough to account for the town's popularity.

Advertisements proclaim that the Palms Grill Café is a step back in time, and that's not mere hyperbole. When you step through the door, the only thing to break the illusion that it's not 1940 or 1950 are the prices. A vintage pinball machine in the corner, black-and-white tile floor, and a board advertising blue-plate specials leave an impression that this is a portal into another time. To sit at the counter and eat a four-dollar fried egg sandwich followed by a slice of freshly baked pie washed down with hot black coffee is about as close to time travel as a person will ever get, especially with big band tunes from World War II gently playing as a backdrop.

110 SW Arch St., Atlanta, IL 61723

www.thepalmsgrillcafe.com

IKE'S CHILI

Will Rogers purportedly quipped that a bowl of chili at Ike's was a "bowl of blessedness." Even though the restaurant has operated at different locations within the city over the years, it remains an institution in Tulsa. Established in 1908, the restaurant's claim to fame is the chili prepared using an original recipe. The menu also features a few traditional diner favorites, but with a twist—jalapeño bacon burger, taco burger, and Frito burrito, to name but a few.

As revitalization sweeps along the 11th Street corridor, an early alignment of Route 66, the locals often share their hometown favorite with travelers from throughout the world. From the stools at the counter to the old-fashioned wooden seats and black-and-white photos on the wall, there's a true sense of timelessness at Ike's.

1503 E. 11th St., Tulsa, OK 74115

www.ikeschilius.com

WILD HARE CAFÉ

This delightful café is representative of the Route 66 renaissance and an era of diversity. The owners, Peter Niehaus from the Netherlands and his wife, Renee Sisk, of South Africa, have lovingly transformed a century-old bank into a place that is almost magical.

The restaurant shares the building with Horsefeathers, a charming antique and gift shop, and Little Foxes, a candy and candle store. Colorful and whimsical murals painted by Sisk adorn the walls of the shop and restaurant. Niehaus has renovated the woodwork and added restored cabinetry salvaged from area demolition projects. This makes for a pleasant setting to enjoy superb dinners and scrumptious desserts. Painting lessons, a lecture series, and a variety of entertainment further ensure that inclusion of the Wild Hare Café in your travel plans will make Elkhart a memorable stop.

104 Governor Oglesby St., Elkhart, IL 62634

www.wildharecafe-elk-il.com

THE BERGHOFF

Dating to 1898, the Berghoff is purportedly the oldest continuously family-operated restaurant on Route 66. Established as a men-only saloon that offered a free corned beef sandwich with the purchase of a ten-cent stein of beer, the facility became a full-service restaurant during Prohibition, offering German American cuisine in a unique ambiance. With the repeal of Prohibition in 1933, the city of Chicago issued liquor license No. 1 to the Berghoff.

Today the Berghoff, located at the heart of the world-famous Loop district, is a social institution in Chicago and a destination for legions of Route 66 enthusiasts. The facility consists of the Berghoff restaurant, the quick-serve, casual dining Berghoff Café, and the historic Berghoff Bar. The Berghoff Restaurant Company of Delaware is owned and operated by Pete Berghoff.

17 W. Adams St., Chicago, IL 60603

www.theberghoff.com

TIP

Exploring Route 66 in major
metropolitan areas can be quite a challenge.
Chicago is no exception. I suggest hiring
a knowledgeable and professional guide to
make this part of the Route 66 adventure more
enjoyable. In Chicago the guide I use is author
David Clark, aka the Windy City Warrior, who
is intimately knowledgeable about the city's
history, its architecture, and hidden gems.

http://windycityroadwarrior.com/

THE FOURWAY

Housed in a colorfully painted 1930s service station and garage complex, this delightful restaurant epitomizes the modern era on Route 66: a repurposed historic building, young owners from the big city in search of the American dream on the Main Street of America, and a menu that blends classic diner food with a modern twist.

As an example, one menu offering is a lamb burger with lettuce, red onion, tomatoes, feta cheese, whole leaf spinach, and tzatziki sauce. Another is flash-fried brussels sprouts drizzled with olive oil, lemon, and balsamic vinaigrette and topped with freshly grated Parmesan cheese. Even the traditional grilled cheese received a tasty upgrade—smoked Gouda and white cheddar on sourdough bread with a garlic pickle spear. For dessert, try baklava or the Farnsworth—fresh vanilla bean ice cream between two chocolate graham crackers topped with fresh strawberries.

102 W. Washington Blvd., Cuba, MO 65453

www.fourway.com

LUCILLE'S ROADHOUSE

A relatively recent newcomer to the Route 66 roadside, this restaurant opened in 2006. However, an argument could be made that its origins date to 1927, the year that Lucille's station and auto court opened a few miles to the east of Weatherford in Hydro. Lucille and Carl Hamons purchased that property in 1941 and remained in business until shortly after the completion of I-40, which bypassed the facility. Lucille received a plaque from the Oklahoma Route 66 Association commemorating fifty-one years in business in 1992, and in 1999 she was inducted into the Oklahoma Route 66 Hall of Fame.

The modern incarnation of Lucille's Roadhouse offers a diverse array of classic favorites as well as local specialties, all served in a time-capsule setting. For breakfast, I suggest beef tips and eggs. If it's lunch or dinner, try the paradise salad or pork stir-fry.

1301 Airport Rd., Weatherford, OK 73096

www.lucillesroadhouse.publishpath.com

BELMONT VINEYARDS

Located on a hill that provides sweeping views of the valley below, the Belmont vineyards, winery, and bistro make for a superb location for a special event or a simple dinner. From the tasting room adorned with European antiques and the work of local artists to the covered porches and the large pavilion, there's an attention to detail that ensures a memorable, relaxed experience. During the annual Cuba Fest in nearby Cuba, the winery figures prominently in the weekend activities with the hosting of evening concerts.

In addition to their signature wines and a new line of "fun wines" that include 90th Anniversary of Route 66 limited editions, the bistro offers some unique dining options made from locally grown ingredients. Spinach and artichoke spread pizza with chicken, bacon, and a three-cheese blend rates as one our favorites, especially with a glass of pink dogwood or edelweiss wine.

5870 Old Route 66, Leasburg, MO 65535

www.belmontvineyards.com

B

BELMONT

VINEYARDS

www.belmont.vineyards.com

BIG VERN'S STEAKHOUSE

The old adage about judging a book by its cover aptly describes Big Vern's Steakhouse. The Lone Star beer, the décor, the dusty and muddy pickup trucks in the parking lot, the menu, the soft drawl of the waitress, and, on occasion, a weathered cowboy at the bar leave little doubt that this is an authentic Texas steakhouse. The food here is pure Americana, and steaks are king of the menu. Still, the offerings are diverse, with a little something for every taste or budget, but my recommendation is the homemade vegetable stew, a cup of coffee, and the cobbler of the day.

Conveniently located within walking distance of the Western Motel, where travelers gather to watch a Texas sunset that gives way to the glow of neon at the historic U-Drop Inn, this wonderful restaurant provides westbound travelers with their first taste of Texas.

200 E. 12th St., Shamrock, TX 79079

www.bigvernssteakhouse.weebly.com

GOLDENLIGHT CAFÉ & CANTINA

Amarillo is a unique Route 66 community. Two of the most famous attractions on this storied old highway (the Big Texan Steak Ranch and the Cadillac Ranch) are located here, and yet neither one is on Route 66. Meanwhile, travelers often overlook the GoldenLight Café & Cantina with its weathered facade on 6th Avenue, the original alignment of Route 66 in Amarillo. Established in 1946, this is the oldest continuously operated restaurant in Amarillo.

On its first day of operation, the menu consisted of hamburgers. Burgers, including buffalo burgers, are still on the menu, but they face stiff competition from green chili burritos, green chili stew (a favorite of mine), and a delicious patty melt. With the addition of the cantina in 1996, live music, cold beer, and great food transformed the venerable old restaurant into a favored hangout for locals.

2908 SW 6th Ave., Amarillo, TX 79106

www.goldenlightcafe.com

ARISTON CAFÉ

The Ariston Café exemplifies the perception that Route 66 is a chain of living, breathing time capsules. Established in 1924 by Pete Adam, a Greek immigrant, this delightful restaurant has operated from the current location since 1935. Even more amazing is the fact that the son of the founder, Nick Adam, and his family now manage the restaurant.

The dining room, the emphasis on customer service, and the personalized attention given by Nick Adam present an impression that here time has stood still for decades. The menu is surprisingly diverse, with entrées that range from steak and pork chops to superb Italian and Mexican dishes, sandwiches, and fresh salads. Desserts prepared on-site, including traditional Greek favorites, round out an excellent meal.

My recommendation is the shepherd's pie, coffee, a slice of pie, and conversation with Nick when he stops at the table to inquire about satisfaction with service.

413 Old Rte. 66 North, Litchfield, IL 62056

www.ariston-cafe.com

PANTRY RESTAURANT

Located along the pre-1937 alignment of Route 66 next to the historic El Rey Inn since 1948, this restaurant has been a favorite of locals, who refer to it as "Santa Fe's Meeting Place," and of travelers who are fortunate enough to discover this little gem.

Even though it's a simple, traditionally styled, family-owned restaurant, it does an incredible amount of business, a testimony to its popularity. According to the restaurant's website, each year it uses three hundred thousand eggs, twenty-six tons of potatoes, and two tons of coffee! Traditional items dominate the menu, but many local favorites hint of the diverse nature of the community: blue corn cinnamon pancakes, huevos consuelo, tortilla burgers, stuffed sopapillas, and a Pantry burger with grilled green chilies, to name but a few.

1820 Cerillos Rd., Santa Fe, NM 87505

www.pantrysantafe.com

KELLY'S BAKERY AND CAFÉ

Coffee shops are not a rarity, but those that blend a unique and pleasant ambiance with tasty treats and intriguing and delightful soups and that are located within walking distance of fascinating historical sites are not overly common.

Examples of the unique menu items include a roasted veggie and hummus stuffed pita, a spicy Italian grilled sandwich, a signature quiche, or portabella ciabatta with basil goat cheese and roasted red peppers. The café also offers excellent fresh specialty soups and gourmet salads with fresh produce. For dessert, consider one of their gourmet cookies or cinnamon rolls and a cup of fresh roasted coffee.

My recommendation? A Black Russian—Angus roast beef, turkey, and provolone cheese in housemade Russian dressing on grilled pumpernickel rye with iced chai.

113 N. Center St., Bloomington, IL 61701

www.kellysbakeryandcafe.com

TIP

While you're in the neighborhood, take a stroll to the McLean County Museum of History, just one block away at 200 North Main Street. Here, housed in the architectural masterpiece that is the 1904 courthouse, you will discover a wide array of fascinating artifacts and collections, including a room dedicated to Abraham Lincoln.

KELLY'S BREW PUB

Housed in the Streamline Moderne–style Ralph Jones Ford dealership built in 1939, Kelly's Brew Pub is a social hub in the century-old Nob Hill district. Listed on the National Register of Historic Places in 1993, the facility served its original purpose until 1957. It housed an army surplus store, a thrift store, and a body shop before Kelly's Brewery purchased the property in 1999.

Though the facility is a restaurant with a children's menu and a full menu of traditional as well as specialty dishes including green chili turkey enchilada cazuela, beer is the focal point of Kelly's Brew Pub, with twenty award-winning house beers on tap. You can even pick a recipe, take lessons, brew your own beer, and come back in two weeks and bottle it!

3222 Central Ave. SE, Albuquerque, NM 87106

www.kellysbrewpub.com

EARL'S FAMILY RESTAURANT

The 10,000-square-foot restaurant opened by Earl Loham was originally a simple burger stand with four stools and two booths. The current owner, Sharon Richards, started as a waitress in 1967 and purchased the business with a handshake in 1972. Popular with locals and travelers alike since 1947, this restaurant offers superb Mexican food as well as traditional American favorites and Native American specialty dishes. A variety of freshly baked pies and cakes and other pastries round out an excellent meal or go well with a simple cup of coffee.

However, what really sets this restaurant apart from others along Route 66 is that it allows vendors. Unless the customer specifies otherwise, Navajo, Zuni, and Hopi artisans approach tables to sell paintings, woven goods, and fine jewelry. This makes for a most interesting dining experience!

1400 Route 66, Gallup, NM 87301

HEIDAR BABA

From its inception, Route 66 reflected the Main Street of America. In the era of renaissance, nothing has changed except the diversity of that main street. Exemplifying this is Heidar Baba, an authentic Persian café whose name is derived from a poem written by Iranian poet Shahriyar.

The owners express this sentiment on their website: "We hope that all of your senses, what you see, what you smell, and of course, what you taste, transport you to the foot of our famous mountain, where you can enjoy the simple pleasures of good food and good conversation, and where your hearts may be gladdened." They accomplish this marvelously through the ambiance and attentive staff, and in the superb and unique menu offerings. My recommendation is the gleimeh bademjoon and doogh to wash it down. However, the kabob plates are also excellent.

1511 E. Colorado Blvd., Pasadena, CA 91106

www.heidarbaba.com

TIP

To round out the Route 66 experience, a blending of the old and new, consider the Saga Motor Hotel two blocks to the east as a lodging choice. Built in 1956, this is a marvelous time capsule, a rare example of the classic California motel with palm-tree-shaded swimming pool.

PINE COUNTRY RESTAURANT

This restaurant, located across the street from the visitors' center housed in the historic freight depot and a few short blocks from the Grand Canyon Railroad, is centrally located. The large windows provide diners with a front-row seat to Route 66 activity.

Pie for breakfast, lunch, or dinner—pies and more pies. That is at the heart of a Pine Country Restaurant experience. With more than thirty-five different delicious varieties to choose from, there's a pie for every taste. Add a visit to the coffee bar, and you have a perfect place to take a break from the road. If you prefer something more substantial, there's an expansive menu for any meal of the day.

For breakfast, my choice is the huevos rancheros, and for lunch I enjoy the Texas red burger. For dinner, I generally have a local favorite, the Navajo taco.

107 N. Grand Canyon Blvd., Williams, AZ 86046

WESTSIDE LILO'S CAFÉ

A dusty old Arizona cattle and railroad town seems an unlikely place to enjoy an authentic German Oktoberfest. An even bigger surprise is the menu offerings at Westside Lilo's: authentic German schnitzel and bratwurst, superb huevos rancheros and chorizo burritos, steak and eggs, fresh carrot cake, and the signature dessert, giant cinnamon rolls. This charming little restaurant is another example of the Route 66 renaissance and how it's transforming communities, as well as what makes the adventure on this storied highway so infectious.

Lilo, a native of Wiesbaden, Germany, and her husband, Patrick, who had lived in Seligman most of his life, opened the restaurant in 1996. The origins of the restaurant, however, date to 1954. With the resurgent interest in Route 66, Lilo's is now a destination, and it's quite popular with European travelers. A stop here should be included in any Route 66 itinerary.

415 Chino St., Seligman, AZ 86337

www.westsidelilos.com

LULU BELLE'S

This restaurant is a relative newcomer to the Route 66 roadside. Still, everything about it captures the essence of the Route 66 experience, from the location and ambiance to the food and staff. As a bonus, the views from the patio are of quintessential western landscapes—mountains and desert plains dotted with junipers.

Barbecue is the restaurant's specialty, and the menu offerings are predominantly traditional American fare. There are, however, a few surprises, especially on the dessert menu. As an example, the cobblers served hot from the oven in a cast-iron skillet and topped with vanilla bean ice cream are superb. Another favorite of ours is the Kick Ass Bourbon Brownie. Either of these go quite well with the Lindermae sandwich, an Angus beef patty on a grilled ciabatta bun with sliced green chili, Swiss cheese, avocado, and sautéed onions with garlic aioli.

33 Lewis Avenue, Ash Fork, AZ 86320

www.lulubellesbbq.com

CLIFTON'S CAFETERIA

Located mere yards from the original western terminus of Route 66 at 7th Street and Broadway in the heart of the historic Los Angeles theater district, Clifton's Cafeteria is more than a mere restaurant—it is a dining experience.

Dating to 1935, this is the world's largest public cafeteria. The interior is a visual delight that is more movie set than restaurant. The main dining hall, Forest Glen, with mineral displays, detailed murals, stepped "stone" terraces, and "trees" supporting the colorful ceiling presents the illusion of dining in a redwood forest. It served as an inspiration to Walt Disney when he was building Disneyland.

The Pacific Seas Tiki Bar continues the theme of whimsy. Rattan and bamboo details, leafy palm fronds, hand-carved wooden sculptures, a built-in wood-paneled speedboat, and a mural of the South Pacific painted by Sammy Beam make for a unique ambiance. Dinner or drinks at Clifton's Cafeteria ensures a very memorable experience.

648 S. Broadway, Los Angeles, CA 90014

www.cliftonsla.com

GRAND CENTRAL MARKET

Dating to 1917, this is the ultimate food court, with vendors and restaurants offering almost any type of drink or food imaginable. Vintage neon signage, bustling crowds speaking dozens of languages, the heady aroma of freshly baked goods and coffee beans roasting, and a labyrinth of stalls and storefronts makes for an almost overwhelming experience. Grand Central Market is a microcosm of the culinary and cultural diversity of the Los Angeles metropolitan area.

Where else on Route 66 can you buy fresh vegetables and exotic fruits, enjoy authentic traditional Japanese and Armenian foods, have a mango and pistachio ice cream cone for dessert, and sip a Turkish coffee in one location? Where else on Route 66 can you enjoy fresh sushi, hop-infused milk shakes, or fresh goat cheese and rye bread sandwiches in the shadow of stunning historic architecture before taking in a classic movie at a century-old theater?

317 S. Broadway, Los Angeles, CA 90013

www.grandcentralmarket.com

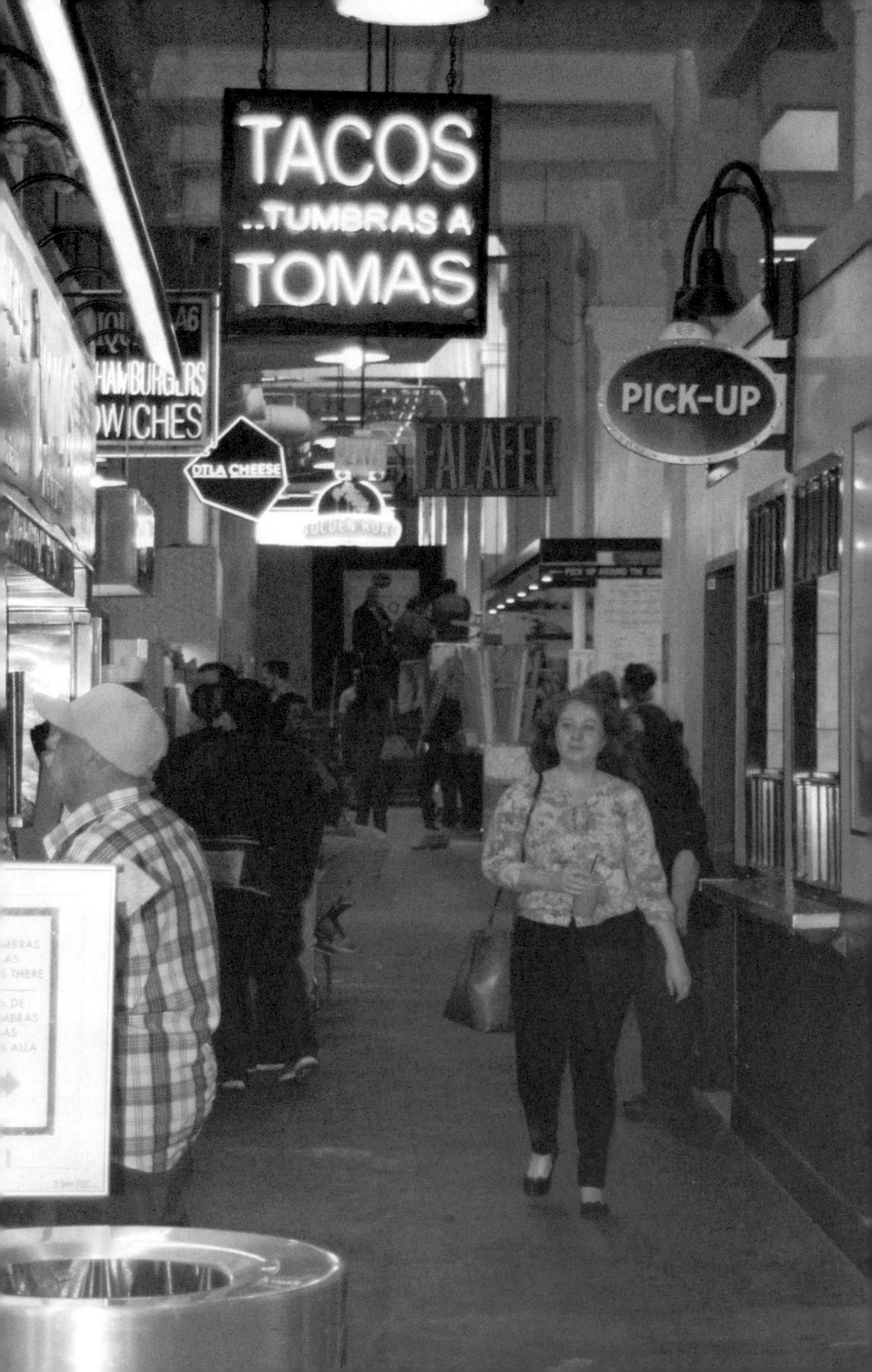
TACOS
..TUMBRAS A
TOMAS
HAMBURGERS
FALAFEL
PICK-UP

FLOYD & COMPANY

Floyd & Company Real Pit BBQ and Floyd & Company Wood-Fired Pizza are housed in the century-old Central Commercial Building. Both offer superb food at reasonable prices, but they are as different as night and day.

The pizzeria has almost a sports-bar ambiance with its stark, simple furnishings that center on the pizza oven. Sidewalk seating is also available. The barbecue restaurant seating is on picnic tables or in booths. Charming touches and historic photographs adorn the walls, and large windows provide a front-row view for events such as Chillin' on Beale or parades. There's an ice cream bar, and a variety of beers from the Black Bridge Brewery across the street are available in both restaurants.

420 Beale St., Kingman, AZ 86401

www.floydandcompany.com

TIP

The historic business district in Kingman, Arizona, is a treasure trove of historic sites, celebrity-associated locations such as the church where Clark Gable and Carol Lombard married, fascinating architecture, neon signs, microbreweries, and eclectic shops. Promote Kingman offers a 2.5-mile, two-hour guided walking tour of the area. Custom tours are also available.

www.promotekingman.com

NEON NIGHTS AND ROOMS WITH A VIEW

COLAW ROOMING HOUSE

The picturesque Colaw Rooming House, built in 1893, is truly a unique dining and lodging experience. Unlike in a traditional bed and breakfast, where you rent a room in a restored Victorian-era home or country manor, in Atlanta you rent the entire house—three bedrooms, a kitchen, bathroom, dining room, parlor, and living room, all filled with period furnishings and renovated vintage appliances.

To ensure guests experience a late 1940s rooming-house experience, attention to detail was the hallmark of the building's restoration. However, to meet the needs of the today's traveler, a few modern touches were added, such as Wi-Fi, flat-screen televisions, a coffee maker, and a microwave oven. As a bonus, if you don't feel like cooking, the wonderful Palms Grill Café, a renovated 1930s-era diner, is a mere two blocks away.

204 NW Vine St., Atlanta, IL 61723

www.thecolawhouse.com

WAGON WHEEL MOTEL

Close your eyes and dream of a row of picturesque stone cabins framed by a park-like setting of shade trees and lawn. Add a touch of vintage neon signage; an old stone service station; a garage that now operates as a gift shop specializing in Route 66 souvenirs, books, and local handicrafts; and an owner who exudes pride of ownership and a passion to ensure customer satisfaction. Next door is a wonderful restaurant known for superb barbecue dinners or lunches served in a charming setting that perfectly captures the rustic, laid-back feel of the Ozark Mountains.

If that's your vision of a wonderful place to enjoy a restful night's sleep or a memorable weekend getaway, then the Wagon Wheel Motel needs to be your destination. Dating to the mid-1930s, this little gem is a tangible link to another era, a time when Route 66 was the Main Street of America.

901 E. Washington Blvd., Cuba, MO 65453

www.wagonwheel66cuba.com

ROADRUNNER LODGE MOTEL

This classic motel is more than just a quaint oasis for the night—it's a place where the traveler can experience a bit of time travel but still enjoy modern amenities.

The west side of the property began as the La Plaza Court in 1947. The east side of the property opened as the state-of-the-art Leatherwood Manor in 1964. Then the older property received an extensive upgrade that included joining both motels under one roof. With the bypass of Route 66 and Tucumcari by I-40, business plummeted. Closure and abandonment followed a few years later.

A unique business model is the foundation for renovations launched by David and Amanda Brenner in 2014. The first stage is transformation of the Leatherwood Manor property to its 1964 appearance, a project that is well under way. The second phase will be the renovation of the La Plaza Court to a 1940s-era appearance, which will result in two historic motels on one property.

1023 E. Rte. 66 Blvd., Tucumcari, NM 88401

www.roadrunnerlodge.com

Las Vegas, New Mexico, is not a Route 66 community. However, as it's located about ten miles from the 1937 alignment, this community is a detour that will really enhance your adventure. Highway 104 is a direct and scenic route from Tucumcari. With more than nine hundred buildings on the National Register of Historic Places, this is a photographer's paradise. The heart of the old town is a charming plaza that predates the Mexican-American War. One of the main streets in this district was the Santa Fe Trail. Dominating the square is the beautifully restored Plaza Hotel, restaurant, and saloon, built in 1882. I would also suggest visiting the Rough Rider Museum. The recruitment drive for Teddy Roosevelt's Rough Riders, and that unit's first reunion, were held at the Plaza Hotel.

MUNGER MOSS MOTEL

Dating to 1946, the Munger Moss Motel has been in the care of Bob and Ramona Lehman since 1971. As careful stewards of the property and passionate pioneers in the Route 66 renaissance movement, the Lehmans ensure that a stay at this iconic motel will be a smile-inducing memory for years to come.

For those struggling to understand why people travel from around the world to drive Route 66, one stay here will answer all their questions. The motel is a delightful blending of the vintage and the modern. It's also a revered treasure. The office, adorned with collectibles as well as gifts given by visitors over the years, is but another indication that this is a very special place. International photographers provided an array of Route 66 images that add color to each room, and period touches exemplify the essence of the Route 66 experience in the modern era.

1336 Rte. 66, Lebanon, MO 65536

www.mungermoss.com

BOOTS COURT MOTEL

The Boots Court Motel is a time capsule that exemplifies the era of renaissance on Route 66. Built in 1939 by Arthur Boots, the complex initially consisted of a service station, now the motel office, and four motel rooms. Since it was the waning years of the Great Depression and Boots was working on a very tight budget, materials utilized in construction included automobile windshields painted to mimic black Carrera glass, handmade furniture, and materials salvaged from area demolition projects. Incredibly, the motel continued to serve travelers until 2001!

Today, with half of the thirteen rooms lovingly restored, "the Boots" is a gem that provides a very immersive lodging experience from the 1940s. The welcoming neon sign has been restored, as has the sign that reads "A Radio in Every Room." Even better, all the rooms feature a radio, no television, refinished wood floors, and period-correct ceramic tile bathrooms.

107 S. Garrison Ave., Carthage, MO 64836

www.bootsmotel.homestead.com

MAYO HOTEL

The Mayo Hotel is an Art Deco masterpiece as well as a stunning monument to historic property renovation. Designed by architect George Winkler, the nineteen-story, 600-room hotel was the tallest building in Tulsa at the time of its opening in 1925. Boasting the most modern amenities and an unparalleled level of luxury in the city, it quickly became the social hub of Tulsa. The lengthy celebrity guest list includes Babe Ruth, Charles Lindbergh, Lucille Ball, Elvis Presley, President John F. Kennedy, J. Paul Getty, and Charlie Chaplin.

Shortly after its listing on the National Register of Historic Places in 1980, the hotel closed. For more than thirty years, it remained vacant and succumbed to neglect as well as vandalism. In 2001, the Snyder family of Tulsa purchased the property, and initiated a $42 million renovation. The hotel reopened in 2009. It is again a social hub in the city and a lodging choice for celebrities, as well as for Route 66 enthusiasts looking for a bit of luxury on their adventure.

115 W 5th St., Tulsa, OK 74103

www.themayohotel.com

BLUE SWALLOW MOTEL

This motel is *the* crown jewel of the Route 66 experience and exemplifies what makes a Route 66 adventure an unforgettable odyssey. Dating to 1939, the motel with its refurbished 1950s neon signage is also perhaps the most photographed nighttime location on the highway. The meticulous attention to detail in the property's renovation and careful addition of modern amenities allow guests to enjoy an almost surreal sense of time travel. Photo opportunities abound in Tucucmari, especially when the sun goes down and the neon lights up the night. One example is the wonderful TeePee Curios sign located across the highway from the Blue Swallow Motel.

Underlying the international passion for traveling Route 66 are the people that give Route 66 an infectious vibrancy and sense of excitement, people such as the Mueller family, proprietors of the Blue Swallow Motel. In addition to the restoration of the property itself, Kevin, Nancy, Cameron, and Jessica strive to ensure that guests become lifelong friends. They also add special touches like serving as chauffeurs in vintage vehicles for local transportation needs, marshmallow roasts in the courtyard, and the occasional mailing of colorful Christmas cards.

815 E. Rte. 66 Blvd., Tucumcari, NM 88401

www.blueswallowmotel.com

HOTEL ANDALUZ

Fully renovated and upgraded, but with an eye on the preservation of unique architectural attributes and an awareness of the historic significance of the hotel, the Andaluz is a wonderful lodging and dining option in Albuquerque. Listed on the National Register of Historic Places in 1984, the hotel opened on June 9, 1939. It was the fourth hotel built by New Mexico native Conrad Hilton. At the time of construction, it was the largest building in the state and the first to offer guests the luxury of air conditioning.

Since completion of the property's renovation and the installation of a rooftop lounge, an array of awards and accolades has been bestowed on the hotel. These include the AAA Four Diamond Award, a listing as one of the top five hotels in the Southwest by *Condé Nast Traveler*, the Earth-Minded Award, and a Heritage Preservation Award.

125 Second St. NW, Albuquerque, NM 87102

www.hotelandaluz.com

EL REY INN

Combine two historic motels, one of which dates to 1936, add a few amenities such as an outdoor fireplace by the hot tub, a heated outdoor pool, laundry facilities, and, in some rooms, fireplaces and kitchenettes. Then set the complex amid a lush and beautiful five-acre garden that's also a bird sanctuary, and you have the delightful El Rey Inn. As a bonus, you are mere minutes, depending on traffic, from the historic Santa Fe Plaza.

Charming touches that exude the feel of the Southwest, with its unique blending of cultures, ensure that each of the eighty-six rooms is different and special. The complex also includes the "lodge," which is ideally suited for families or small groups. In addition to a full kitchen and gas-lit fireplace, the lodge also features a private glass-enclosed porch, one and a half bathrooms, and two great rooms.

1862 Cerrillos Rd., Santa Fe, NM 87505

www.elreyinnsantafe.com

SUNSET MOTEL

Recently, motels that have an historic association with Route 66 topped the list of endangered properties along that highway. Now, just imagine how rare it is to find a one-family-owned motel that dates to 1954!

Bill Pogue was well acquainted with the motel business, since his mother operated the Yucca Auto Court in Moriarty. With his wife, Elaine, and plans drawn on a brown paper bag, Bill initiated construction on a project that would continue until 1969 and result in a fifteen-room complex. Shortly after Bill's untimely death, Elaine sold the motel to their son Mike. He and his wife, Debbie, continue to operate the motel.

If travelers are looking for the Hilton experience, they will be sorely disappointed. If, however, they are looking for clean, basic lodging and friendly, smiling owners, as well as a vintage experience, the Sunset Motel will fit the bill quite nicely.

501 E. Rte. 66, Moriarty, NM 87035

www.sunseton66.com

MONTERREY NON-SMOKERS MOTEL

Centrally located near the Old Town District, as well as the zoo and other attractions, this roadside gem is a lodging bargain and a clean, well-maintained classic that has origins as a 1946 auto court. Well into the 1960s, the property evolved to meet the changing needs of the traveler, and today the AAA-rated, three-star property features a swimming pool and laundry facilities.

In 1954, the *Western Accommodation Directory* published by AAA noted that amenities included air-cooled units, individually controlled vented heat, and tiled showers and that radios were available. Rates ranged from four to six dollars per night. The property still garners favorable reviews, and in the third edition of *Route 66: EZ66 Guide for Travelers,* author Jerry McClanahan noted that it was his favorite lodging choice in Albuquerque.

2402 Central Ave. SW, Albuquerque, NM 87104

www.nonsmokersmotel.com

Old Town Albuquerque is one of our must-stop sites when we drive Route 66. The crowds, the street performers, the artists, the restaurants, and the business owners exude an infectious vibrancy and enthusiasm. La Placita restaurant is housed in the oldest building in the district. It was built as a hacienda in 1706, and a second-story addition was built in 1872. The San Filipe de Neri Church dates to 1793. As early as 1632, several families had established a rancheria at the site. The roots of the city's historic heart, however, are even older. An expedition in 1540 noted the ruins of a village at the site.

EL RANCHO HOTEL

The charming and quirky El Rancho Hotel is dated and a bit worn at the heel. However, since it's an almost perfectly preserved 1940s-era five-star resort that served as an oasis for dozens of movie stars and celebrities, it's easy to overlook the shortcomings. Attesting to its former glory is the mezzanine, which has a gallery of signed photos from the rich and famous that have stayed here over the years.

Billed as the world's largest ranch house at its opening, the architecture inside and out is rather unique. On-site are Ortega's Jewelry Store, one part gift shop and one part Native American art gallery; the 49er Lounge; and a wonderful restaurant that offers superb Mexican food as well as regional specialties such as atole, a Native American blue cornmeal mush. This hotel is more than a haven for the weary traveler—it's a memory-making experience.

1000 E. Hwy. 66, Gallup, NM 87301

www.elranchohotel.com

ENCHANTED TRAILS RV PARK & TRADING POST

Dating to the 1940s, this charming and unique lodging option opened as a trading post near the summit of Nine Mile Hill west of Albuquerque. At one point in its history, the realignment of Route 66 necessitated the dismantling of the structure and rebuilding it on the other side of the new highway.

Today the original building serves as an office and houses a gift shop and a laundry for RV park guests. However, what really sets this place apart from any other lodging on Route 66 is the vintage travel trailers that serve as motel rooms and a few cars from the same period that make for excellent photo ops, especially at sunset. The trailers do have a few modern touches, but for the most part they are period correct right down to the vintage refrigerators and radios. The trailers-turned-motel-rooms include a 1969 Airstream, a 1956 Yellowstone, a 1959 Spartan, and a 1963 Winnebago.

14305 Central Ave. NW, Albuquerque, NM 87121

www.enchantedtrails.com

GLOBETROTTER LODGE

An apt description of the charming Globetrotter Lodge in Holbrook is that it is a delightful roadside gem where the past and present blend seamlessly. The motel's appearance presents the impression that time has stood still, but that's a mere illusion, since it has undergone a wide array of changes since opening in the late 1950s. In fact, at one point demolition seemed imminent.

Now, however, the cozy ten-room motel is a delightful blend of historic roadside oasis, charming artistic touches such as Mexican ceramic mural sinks, and a setting for breakfast that mimics a quaint European café. Peter and Mona, formerly of Austria, have effected this wonderful transformation with hard work, attention to detail, and a level of personal service usually found in five-star resorts.

902 W. Hopi Dr., Holbrook, AZ 86025

www.hotelsholbrookaz.com

SAGA MOTOR HOTEL

The Saga Motor Hotel is a rare urban survivor, a delightful time capsule that exudes an atmosphere of 1950s California. The tall palm trees that cast shadows over the heated pool—as well as the courtyard, the office, the lobby, and even the pink stucco walls—present the illusion that at this motel, time stopped in 1958. Yet guests can also enjoy the expected modern amenities: a free continental breakfast, business center, secure parking, free laundry facilities, Wi-Fi, and flat-screen HD televisions.

Dating to 1956, the motel is conveniently located within walking distance of an array of fascinating and diverse restaurants, as well as a station for the excellent urban light rail system that provides quick access to downtown Los Angeles or points west as far as Santa Monica. My recommendation is to ask for a ground-floor room, preferably poolside, and a local restaurant guide.

1633 E. Colorado Blvd., Pasadena, CA 91106

www.thesagamotorhotel.com

When it opened in 1925, the Aztec Hotel located at 311 West Foothill Boulevard in Monrovia, California, was so architecturally unique that an entire movement was launched. The Beach & Yacht Club in La Jolla, California; the Mayan Hotel in Kansas City, Missouri; and the Mayan Theater in Los Angeles were patterned after the hotel designed by Robert Stacy-Judd. Additionally, several companies formed to produce fixtures, tiles, and even furniture that mimicked items found at the Aztec Hotel. The building faces an uncertain future, which should make it a must-stop photo op.

Missouri History Museum—Forest Park (page 8)

The Arcade Museum—Palms Grill Café (page 30)

Route 66 Fun Run (page 160)

Devils Elbow (page 112)

Albuquerque Old Town Distri

The FourWay (page 36)

Cyrus Avery Centennial Plaza (page 119)

Grand Canyon Caverns (page 156)

Sitgreaves Pass (page 123)

Chevelon Canyon Bridge (page 120)

Two Guns, Arizona (page 118)

World's Second Largest Rocking Chair (page 129)

FENDER'S RIVER ROAD RESORT & MOTEL

Fender's, as the website says, is a "funky 1960's-era resort" located on Route 66 and the National Old Trails Highway that fronts the Colorado River. As a result, it's the only property of its kind in California. The motel is dated but in a quaint manner. Modern amenities including air conditioning, a must when summertime temperatures rise above 120 degrees, ensure a pleasant stay. The 31-space RV park is often a haven for snowbirds, the name for people who flee colder climates to winter along the Colorado River. Riverfront campsites for those who prefer roughing it in style are also available.

For Route 66 enthusiasts, the property is ideally suited as a base for exploration to Oatman, Goffs, and Needles. In addition, for those who enjoy some exciting nightlife, the casinos of Laughlin, Nevada, are just a few miles upriver.

3396 Needles Hwy., Needles, CA 92363

www.fendersresort.com

LA POSADA HOTEL

The La Posada is a delightful blending of the vision of Mary Elizabeth Jane Colter, the original architect, and the passion of current owner Allan Affeldt. Colter expanded on the mission style popular in the 1920s and created a romanticized illusion that this hotel and its grounds comprised a weathered Spanish ranchero. To accomplish this, she made extensive use of adobe, stucco, exposed ceiling beams, sandblasted planks for doors and window shutters, stone, wrought iron, terra-cotta tile, and flagstone. When Affeldt restored the property, he did so with respect for Colter's work, as well as a bit of artistic license, since he was working with a blank slate.

After closure of the restaurant in 1956 and the hotel in 1959, the Santa Fe Railroad gutted the complex and transformed it into offices and then slated it for demolition shortly before Affeldt acquired the property in 1997. Today the La Posada consistently rates as one of the nation's premier historic railroad hotels and is a destination for travelers in northern Arizona.

303 E. 2nd St., Winslow, AZ 86047

www.laposada.org

MEMORY-MAKING PHOTO STOPS

WILLIS TOWER

For a truly unique view of Route 66 and a one-of-a-kind photo opportunity, look no further than the Skydeck glass bays at the Willis Tower, formerly the Sears Tower. At 1,353 feet above the street, on a clear day visitors can see four states as well as the Route 66 corridor coursing across Chicago in a manmade canyon of steel and concrete. The 103rd floor also houses an array of interactive exhibits about the building's construction and a café, as well as the Skydeck Marketplace.

Deemed an engineering marvel at the time of its construction, it remained the world's tallest building until 1998. Ongoing renovations and upgrades are transforming the building into an innovative leader in the use of alternative energy as well as conservation programs. In two decades, the annual electrical consumption has decreased by 34 percent.

233 S. Wacker Dr., Chicago, IL 60606

www.willistower.com

Another location ideally suited for the photographer with an interest in historic architecture is the Riverside Landscape Architecture District bordered by alignments of Route 66 on Harlem and Ogden Avenues west of Chicago. This national historic landmark is a remnant of the original village of Riverside, one of America's first planned communities. It was designed by city planner Frederick Law Olmstead, best known as the creator of New York City's Central Park. In this district, you'll find buildings designed by a number of famous architects including Frank Lloyd Wright and Daniel Burnham.

MURALS ON MAIN STREET

Dominated by the beautiful nineteenth-century courthouse, the historic core of Pontiac is a paradise for photographers. Accentuating the charming details of the various historic buildings are delightful, colorful murals, even in the alleys. In 2009, the Walldogs, a group of sign painters and muralists, completed eighteen of the twenty murals in just four days during a painting marathon. The most famous of these is the Route 66 shield mural on the rear of the Route 66 Museum, which recently graced the cover of a National Geographic Society calendar.

Most of the murals are portrayals of moments in the city's history or reproductions of advertisements. The 3-D sidewalk shark mural completed by Chinese artist Tang Dongbai in 2012 adds a whimsical touch to a mural walk through the community's historic business district.

Pontiac, IL 61764

www.visitpontiac.org

CHAIN OF ROCKS BRIDGE

For safety reasons, it's best to access the historic Chain of Rocks Bridge from the Illinois side of the river. Built in 1929, the 5,353-foot cantilever through truss bridge with a unique 22-degree bend in the middle is a delightful photo stop, especially during the months of early fall when the shore is lined with colorful foliage. However, as the bridge also provides the visitor with interesting views of St. Louis and the Mississippi River, photo opportunities are limited only by the imagination.

At the time of construction, it served as a toll bridge for those wishing to bypass the congestion of urban St. Louis. Beginning in 1936, the bridge carried traffic as U.S. 66A ("A" for alternate route), a city bypass. It continued to carry traffic despite its narrow roadbed until 1967.

Between St. Louis, MO, and Madison, IL

www.nps.gov/nr/travel/route66/chain_of_rocks_bridge_
illinois_missouri.html

RED BRICK ROAD

This photo op is a bit unusual in that the road itself is the attraction, and the rolling landscapes serve as the frame. There are two sections of road here, each representing different eras of highway engineering.

The 1,277-foot section of sixteen-foot-wide Portland cement dates to 1921, five years before certification of U.S. 66. A 1.53-mile section of this original roadbed overlaid by hand with red bricks in 1932 carried Route 66 traffic until realignment later that year. Originally, this was State Route 4. Known as the Auburn Brick Road, this section of the original alignment of Route 66 also contains two original single-span bridges dating to 1920, both of which make delightful backdrops for photographing the bucolic setting.

Auburn, IL 62615

www.nps.gov/nr/travel/route66/illinois_road_segments.html

Near Chatham, Illinois—nestled between the original alignment of Route 66, State Highway 4, and the last alignment that parallels I-55—is the Sugar Creek Covered Bridge. This is one of five historic covered bridges in the state. From either alignment, it's less than a three-mile detour. Built in 1880, the restored sixty-foot bridge is the focal point of scenic Pioneer Park. The park derives its name from the site of Robert Pullman's homestead established in 1817. During the months of summer, the park is an ideal location for enjoying a picnic. With the arrival of fall colors, the park and bridge are a wonderful place for a photo op.

MOJAVE NATIONAL PRESERVE

Towering sand dunes that seem to sing with desert breezes framed by stark desert mountains, volcanic cinder cones, Joshua tree forests, and carpets of wildflowers during the months of spring are a few of the gems found in this 1.6-million-acre park. Miles of trails lead to canyons, mountains, and mesas that provide stunning viewpoints. Long-abandoned mines and homesteads and even the ruins of a rock-walled military outpost on the historic Mojave Road provide unlimited photo opportunities.

The park headquarters is in Barstow, but the visitor center is at the ghost town of Kelso in the 1924 train station. The renovated Kelso Depot reopened in 2005. Former dormitory rooms contain an array of exhibits describing the cultural and natural history of the area. The baggage room, ticket office, and two dormitory rooms have been historically furnished to illustrate life in the depot in the first half of the twentieth century. A twenty-minute orientation film is shown in the theater.

2701 Barstow Road, Barstow, CA 92311

www.nps.gov/moja

ROUTE 66 MURAL CITY

Amply sprinkled through this charming community in the Ozark Mountains are more than twelve expansive, colorful, and detailed murals chronicling the town's history, which includes Civil War battles, the first Model T Ford in town, and a visit by Bette Davis. The murals are the cornerstone for a surprisingly diverse and imaginative citywide beautification project that includes gardens as well as pocket parks and even brightly painted old bicycles.

The murals are not limited to the business district and Route 66 corridor. In the Crawford County History Museum, a former school located at 308 North Smith Street, murals capture the feel of the 1950s high school experience. One of the things that makes these murals unique is the incorporation of items such as a storage closet door painted to look like a bookcase.

Cuba, MO 65453

www.cubamurals.com

CROSS OF OUR LORD JESUS CHRIST

The cross at Groom, Texas, purported to be the tallest in the United States, dominates the horizon for miles during the drive on Route 66 across the Panhandle. When illuminated at night, as a beacon it's impossible to miss. Initial plans called for the construction of a large billboard, but before construction could commence, the project morphed into a vision for the creation of a monument of epic proportions.

The nineteen-story cross was built in two welding shops in Pampa, Texas, and 2.5 million pounds of steel were used in its construction! In addition, the surrounding park includes life-size bronze sculptures depicting the Stations of the Cross and an empty stone tomb to represent the promise of the resurrection. There's also a memorial for the unborn, a life-size depiction of the Last Supper in bronze, a gift shop, a fountain, paintings by Kenneth Wyatt, and a bronze statue of Saint Michael.

Exit 112, I-40, Groom, TX 79039

www.crossministries.net

TIP

If you enjoy visiting unique religious sites, consider a stop in Benld, Illinois. Located here is the Holy Dormition of the Theotokos, the only Russian Orthodox parish under the Moscow Patriarchate in Illinois. Built in 1915, the charming church was renovated in 1989.

DEVILS ELBOW

In 1941, the state of Missouri's planning commission listed seven beauty spots, and the Devils Elbow on the Big Piney River made the list. The scenic beauty of the area still makes this a delightful photo op. However, there's so much more, including the hamlet of Devils Elbow, the steel truss bridge built over the Big Piney River in 1923, and a picturesque railroad bridge. The backdrop of fall colors ensures beautiful photos.

Then there's the quirky and photogenic Elbow Inn & BBQ, a historic roadhouse that started as the Munger Moss sandwich shop in 1936, with its interesting interior decorations. For reasons unknown, many years ago women began donating brassieres. By the hundreds, these now adorn the ceiling as curvaceous stalactites.

Devils Elbow, MO

roadtripusa.com/route-66/missouri/old-route-66-devils-elbow/

BRUSH CREEK BRIDGE

Located between Galena and Baxter Springs on the 13.5 miles of Route 66 in Kansas is the graceful sweep of Brush Creek Bridge. Built in 1923, the bridge carried Route 66 traffic into the mid-1960s. Utilizing the unique Marsh Arch design, the bridge is a rarity, since only approximately thirty-five of this type remain. James Barney Marsh, a bridge engineer in Iowa, patented the design in 1912. There were three bridges of this type on Route 66 in Kansas, but demolition of the others served as a catalyst for preservation initiatives.

The bridge is one of the most photographed locations on Route 66 in Kansas. It's also a popular site for weddings and special events. In 2000, singer Brad Paisley performed the song "Route 66" on the bridge for a Learning Channel special titled *Route 66: Main Street of America.*

SE Beasley Rd., Baxter Springs, KS 66713

U-DROP INN

The animated film *Cars* led to the U-Drop Inn's becoming one of the most recognized landmarks on Route 66. The complex opened in 1936 as the Tower Service Station and U-Drop Inn Restaurant. Built with extensive use of brick and green-glazed tile and trimmed with colorful neon, advertisements proclaimed that this was the "swankiest of swank eating places" and "the most up-to-date edifice of its kind on U.S. Highway 66 between Oklahoma City and Amarillo."

In 2003 and 2004, with funding that included a $1.7 million federal grant, the entire facility was restored to its original appearance. Owned by the city of Shamrock, it currently houses a museum and a visitors' center with a gift shop. Route 66 enthusiasts from around the world plan their trips so they're in Shamrock at night to photograph the colorfully lit landmark.

1242 N. Main St., Shamrock, TX 79079

www.shamrockedc.org

GLENRIO

The empty four-lane highway with prairie grass growing in the cracks, a few long-closed businesses, and a faint hum of traffic on the interstate highway to the north make a visit to Glenrio a haunting and memorable experience. This forlorn old ghost town that straddles the New Mexico–Texas state line is also, surprisingly, a destination for legions of photographers and Route 66 enthusiasts.

In the late 1910s, Glenrio was a thriving farming community that supported a hotel, newspaper, railroad station, and hardware store. Certification of U.S. 66 fueled expansion of the business district that soon included cafés, garages, and assorted stores. In 1975, the interstate highway bypassed the town, and in twelve months most businesses closed. The highway in town and seventeen abandoned buildings were listed on the National Register of Historic Places in 2007. One of these is the former Texas Longhorn Restaurant and Motel that had a sign reading "Last Motel in Texas" on one side and "First Motel in Texas" on the opposite side.

Exit 0, I-40, Texas–New Mexico state line

www.nps.gov/nr/travel/route66/glenrio_historic_district.html

Except for the last few miles at the west side of the state where the plains give way to the broken Cap Rock country, in Texas the course of Route 66 is across gently rolling hills and featureless plains. That contrast makes the sensory delight that is Palo Duro Canyon State Park, "the Grand Canyon of Texas," even more overwhelming. Located a few miles south of Amarillo, the park opened on July 4, 1934, and contains 29,182 acres that constitute the northernmost portion of the Palo Duro Canyon. Most of the buildings and roads still in use were created by the Civilian Conservation Corps of the 1930s. The canyon is 120 miles long, 20 miles wide in some places, and has a depth of 800 feet. The state of Texas claims that Palo Duro Canyon is the second-largest canyon in the United States, exceeded only by the Grand Canyon of Arizona. The abundant forest of juniper and mesquite trees led early Spanish explorers to name the canyon "Palo Duro," which is Spanish for "hard wood."

TWO GUNS, ARIZONA

Don't let the graffiti-covered ruins of the campground at the interstate highway exit fool you. Two Guns is a photographer's paradise, an almost magical place with a storied history. Accessed via the frontage road that once served as Route 66, just a few hundred yards west of the old campground are the Apache Death Caves, the ruins of a service station, and a weathered stone facade with a sign that reads "Mountain Lions," which frames the sun-bleached remnants of a century of businesses catering to tourists at Canyon Diablo.

The canyon itself provides endless opportunities for capturing stunning scenes, especially if the San Francisco Peaks that dominate the western horizon are covered in snow. In addition, using the canyon as a backdrop for photos of the ruins of Rimmy Jim Giddings's trading post or the 1915 National Old Trails Highway Bridge that spans the canyon multiplies that opportunity a thousandfold.

Between Meteor Crater and Winona
Exit 230, I-40
Coconino County, AZ

CYRUS AVERY CENTENNIAL PLAZA

Cyrus Avery Centennial Plaza, dedicated to Cyrus Avery, the "Father of Route 66," represents stage one of an expansive project that will transform this section of the city. The flags of the eight states through which Route 66 passes fly over the plaza on the banks of the Arkansas River. The Skywalk, designed to mimic the style of the Art Deco period, provides an opportunity to photograph the plaza with a bird's-eye view. The centerpiece of the plaza is the 135-percent-of-actual-size *East Meets West* sculpture, created by Robert Summers, which depicts the Avery family in a 1926 Ford startling the team of horses pulling an oil field wagon.

The stunning detail of the sculpture will keep the photographer busy for hours. For example, there's a smashed grasshopper on the radiator grille of the Model T, and the teamster's boot has a hole in it. The license plate on the Ford reads "Tulsa Route 66 1927."

Southwest Blvd., Tulsa, OK 74127

www.vision2025.com

CHEVELON CANYON BRIDGE

Chevelon Canyon Bridge never carried Route 66 traffic. However, it did carry the traffic of the National Old Trails Highway, predecessor of U.S. 66, and since I-40 construction erased much of Route 66 between Holbrook and Winslow, this makes for a very scenic detour. The bridge, and the canyon it spans are nothing short of stunning.

The bridge is also historically significant because it was one of the first highway projects authorized by the newly formed state of Arizona. On October 2, 1912, the state awarded a $4,985 contract to the Missouri Valley Bridge & Iron Works to span the chasm. In July 1913, the Warren pony truss bridge officially opened. In 2013, the state of Arizona initiated a complete renovation of the bridge that included rebuilding the footing and replacing the deck.

Territorial and Laws Road between Holbrook and Winslow
Navajo County, AZ

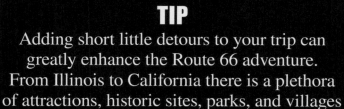

TIP

Adding short little detours to your trip can greatly enhance the Route 66 adventure. From Illinois to California there is a plethora of attractions, historic sites, parks, and villages awaiting discovery. If possible, keep your schedule flexible and always talk with the locals about area attractions or events.

COLORADO STREET BRIDGE

Fortunately, there are numerous ways to access the Colorado Street Bridge, allowing the photographer to shoot this stunning architectural masterpiece that dates to 1913 from numerous angles. Designed by John Drake Mercereau, the bridge curves 50 degrees to the south. Proclaimed the highest concrete bridge in the world upon completion, the graceful arches that stand 150 feet above the Arroyo Seco frame surprisingly lush landscapes in this urban setting. In spite of the narrow 25-foot roadway, the bridge carried Route 66 traffic until 1940.

Deemed a Historic Civil Engineering Landmark, the bridge garnered further recognition with a listing in the National Register of Historic Places in 1981. The bridge closed in 1989 but reopened in 1993 after completion of a $27 million renovation. To enhance your photo op, plan to visit during the annual summer festival on the bridge.

Pasadena, CA 91105

www.nps.gov/nr/travel/route66/colorado_street_bridge_pasadena.html

SITGREAVES PASS

Often referred to as the most scenic segment of Route 66, the pre-1952 alignment of Route 66 through Sitgreaves Pass in the Black Mountains of western Arizona features a series of hairpin curves and steep grades. Quintessential Western landscapes of stone spires, deep canyons, and breathtaking views make this section of Route 66 a photographer's dream. Enhancing the natural beauty are picturesque ruins, lovingly rebuilt roadside businesses, and the sunbaked remnants of a ghost town.

The sense of history in the pass is palpable. Father Garces camped at Little Meadows, now Ed's Camp, in 1776. The original alignment of the nineteenth-century Beale Wagon Road is in this narrow pass, and in 1914 Louis Chevrolet, Barney Oldfield, and other drivers raced along the National Old Trails Highway over this pass in the last of the Desert Classic automobile races.

East of Oatman, AZ

PETRIFIED FOREST NATIONAL PARK

Petrified Forest National Park, which also includes large swaths of the Painted Desert, is the only national park bisected by Route 66. In addition to being one of the most scenic sections of the highway, it's also the most difficult to access, since many miles are only open to the public once a year in June as part of the nearby Holbrook Route 66 Festival. The former Painted Desert Inn that now serves as the visitor center and museum is, however, an excellent photo stop.

Originally built in 1924 at a site that provided expansive views of the stunning landscapes, it was sold to the National Park Service in 1935. Extensive expansion and remodeling transformed the complex, and in 1940, after the Fred Harvey Company leased the property and hired acclaimed architect Mary Jane Colter to oversee the project, it underwent the modifications that resulted in its current appearance.

www.nps.gov/pefo/index.htm

This little photo op will require a short but fun detour. A project to honor pioneer women initiated in 1909 by the Daughters of the American Revolution gained a valuable partner in 1912. In that year, the National Old Trails Road Association included a promise of assistance in their bylaws. Initially the concept was simply to commemorate pioneering mothers who traversed the nation in the eighteenth and nineteenth century with cast-iron markers. In 1924, Mrs. John Trigg Moss, chair of the national DAR committee, submitted plans for a series of statues created by August Leimbach of St. Louis. The statues were to be erected in each of the twelve states through which the National Old Trails Highway passed. With certification of Route 66 in November, sections of this pioneering highway in New Mexico, Arizona, and California were used for the new highway. As a result, two of the statues are located on Route 66, one in Albuquerque and the other in Upland, California. The Arizona statue is in Springerville near Holbrook. A short but scenic drive through the Painted Desert is required if you want to photograph this monument to pioneering women.

COOL SPRINGS

Towering stone buttes and vast fields of black volcanic rock amply peppered with cacti as a backdrop make it difficult to take a bad photograph at Cool Springs. During the winter months, the snow-covered Hualapai Mountains that loom over the broad Sacramento Valley provide a study in contrasts. A short but steep hiking trail that twists to the top of a stone palisade opposite Cool Springs enhances the photographic opportunities.

Originally built in 1926, the stone-faced complex evolved to meet increasing traffic needs. By the mid-1930s, it consisted of a series of cabins, a restaurant, and a service station. In 1965, fire devastated the entire complex. In 1991, a movie set was built around the ruins and blown up for the movie *Universal Soldier.* Ned Leutchner acquired the property in 1997 and commenced construction of a museum and gift shop that mimicked the 1930s appearance of Cool Springs.

Between Kingman and Oatman, AZ

www.route66coolspringsaz.com

TIP

If you're traveling Route 66 through Kingman, Arizona, in the summer, a respite from the heat is a mere twelve scenic miles to the south. Hualapai Mountain Park and Hualapai Mountain Lodge are in the Hualapai Mountains, a pine-covered oasis surrounded by desert. The park features miles of pine-shaded trails that lead to scenic viewpoints, rustic cabins, and campsites. The lodge offers fine dining and overnight accommodations at the motel. Dusk or early evening are the best times to visit the lodge as elk are often seen in the parking lot.

BLUE HOLE

Located along an early alignment of Route 66 on the south side of Santa Rosa, this wonderful park is truly an oasis, a sparkling blue gem in a sea of desert. The centerpiece of this charming roadside park (bring your picnic basket), is the Blue Hole, with water so clear that there's visibility to the hundred-foot level. The springs are two hundred feet deep.

A constant year-round 62-degree water temperature makes it ideal for a summer swim. What really sets this park apart from others along Route 66 and in the Southwest is that it's also a scuba diving destination and a diving training facility. The diving training facility offers an array of amenities. These include a warm room with showers, dive shop with supplies, three underwater training platforms, tank refills, and equipment rentals.

Santa Rosa, NM

www.santarosabluehole.com

WORLD'S SECOND LARGEST ROCKING CHAIR

Quirky Route 66 attractions have always been an integral part of an adventure on this storied highway. That trend continues unabated in the era of renaissance.

Located four miles west of Cuba, Missouri, next to the closed Fanning Route 66 Outpost, is a bright red, 42-foot rocking chair. Erected on April Fool's Day, 2008, the project was the brainchild of Dan Sanazaro, owner of the store at the time. The inspiration for the creation came from his fond memory of seeing something similar on a family road trip as a child, as well as a desire to eclipse the record held by Big John, a giant rocking chair in Franklin, Indiana.

Once a year, on Picture on Rocker Day, held the first Saturday in August, visitors can have their photos taken in the seat. Comedian Billy Connolly added to the chair's fame during the filming of his Route 66 travel series.

5957 Hwy. ZZ, Fanning, MO

www.visitmo.com/worlds-largest-rocking-chair.aspx

ROY'S

Incredibly, the forlorn and weathered oasis that is Roy's in Amboy, a ghost town in the Mojave Desert, is one of the most photographed locations on Route 66. Even more amazing, it has served as a shooting location for commercials to market a diverse array of products including Australian insurance, Japanese beer, German clothing, and even automobiles. The complex consists of a service station, the only operational business; a long-closed motel; and a non-operational café.

Framing the forlorn oasis are stark but stunning desert landscapes. One of the most prominent is Amboy Crater, a long-dormant volcano. Other buildings in Amboy include a post office, a long-closed school and church, and a few old houses.

87520 National Trails Hwy., Amboy, CA 92304

www.rt66roys.com

Ghost town exploration adds a bit of context to the Route 66 adventure. It also provides an opportunity to get out of the car for a bit and to stretch the legs. Always be respectful of private property, obey trespassing signs, and watch for snakes. Adhere to the adage about taking nothing but photographs and leaving nothing but footprints. Romeroville, New Mexico, on the pre-1937 alignment of Route 66 north of Santa Rosa, is a wonderful place to discover the thrill of ghost town exploration. The namesake for the faded village is Don Trinidad Romero, a member of the Territory of New Mexico House of Representatives in 1863, a congressional representative for the territory from 1877 to 1879, a probate judge, and a marshal. His home, now gone, was visited by General William Tecumseh Sherman and President Rutherford B. Hayes.

SANTA MONICA PIER

Technically, the pier is not on Route 66. The western terminus of the highway is located several blocks to the east. Still, the pier that opened in 1909 has served as the traditional end for at least eighty years, and who will make the drive from Chicago and not at least see the ocean?

Photo opportunities, as well as the opportunity for sensory overload, abound on the historic pier. From the "End of the Trail" sign, a replicated movie prop, to the Last Stop Shop with its Bob Waldmire memorial exhibit at the end of the pier, this is a great souvenir photo stop for the Route 66 enthusiast. Add quirky restaurants, street performers, and a vintage amusement park with a few modern touches, and you have the perfect place to end an adventure on Route 66.

Santa Monica, CA 90401

www.santamonicapier.org

There are enough attractions along Route 66 from San Bernardino to Santa Monica to fill several vacations. However, traffic in the greater Los Angeles metropolitan area can be quite intimidating. As a result, many enthusiasts bypass this corridor and utilize the freeway to access the traditional western end of Route 66 at Santa Monica Pier. My suggestion is to drive the section from San Bernardino to Pasadena on Saturday. Traffic along Foothill and Colorado Boulevard, the primary course of Route 66, is relatively light, but it's a seemingly endless string of traffic lights. Early Sunday morning is the best time to drive from Pasadena into the historic business district of Los Angeles. Even though traffic is lighter on weekends, driving through Hollywood, Beverly Hills, and Santa Monica requires patience and time. As with Chicago, a knowledgeable and professional guide can enhance your exploration of the Route 66 corridor in Los Angeles. My recommendation is author and guide Scott Piotrowski.

http://www.route66losangeles.com/about.html

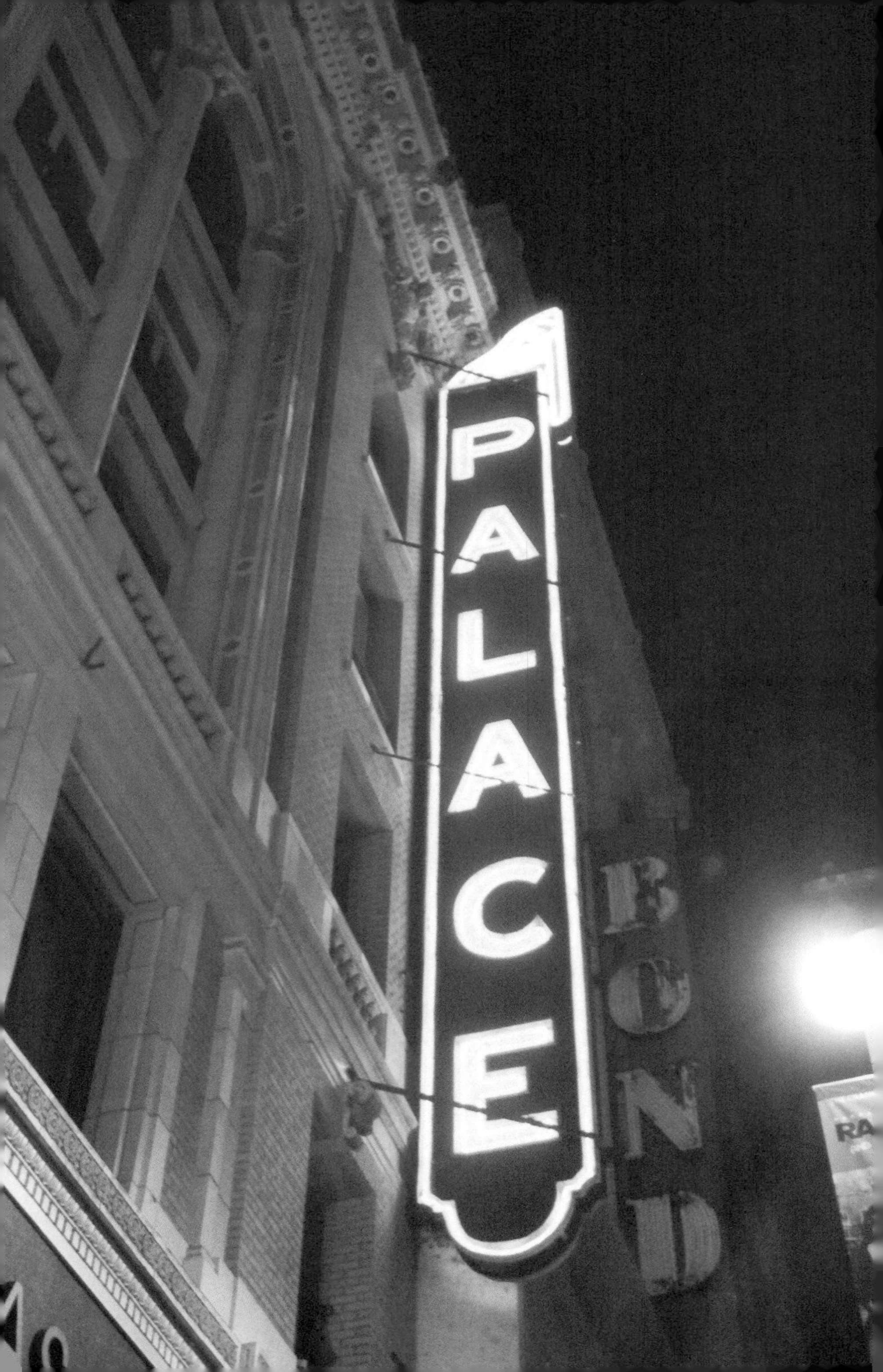
PALACE
BOND

MUST-SEE ATTRACTIONS

GRANT PARK

Renamed to honor President Ulysses S. Grant in 1901, the 319-acre Grant Park, referred to as "Chicago's front yard," anchors the eastern terminus of Route 66. It dates to 1835. Located within the park are Millennium Park, Buckingham Fountain, Adler Planetarium, Shedd Aquarium, and the Art Institute of Chicago. Annually, the park is the site for many large events, including Taste of Chicago and the Grant Park Music Festival.

Between 1998 and 2004, work transformed the western edge of the park into Millennium Park, with artistic features, and Daley Bicentennial Plaza became a lakefront recreation center that included an ice skating ribbon with renovations completed in 2015. Built in 1893, the Art Institute of Chicago is one of the nation's premier art facilities, and Buckingham Fountain, added to the park in 1927, appears in the opening credits of the television program *Married . . . with Children.*

337 E. Randolph St., Chicago, IL 60601

www.chicagoparkdistrict.com

TIP

The Museum of Natural History in Chicago should be included as a stop on any Route 66 odyssey. One of the exhibits has an interesting Route 66 connection. On March 29, 1938, a meteorite passed through Edward McCain's garage roof and his 1928 Pontiac coupe. Portions of the car and the meteorite are on display at the museum.

ROUTE 66 BLUE CARPET CORRIDOR FESTIVAL/ RED CARPET CORRIDOR FESTIVAL

The Route 66 Blue Carpet Corridor Festival that takes place in mid-June is an event that celebrates the unique nature of Route 66 and the communities along that highway corridor in southern Illinois between Virden and Collinsville. The festival showcases towns and villages, as well as their rich mining history and links to legends of mob association. Each community hosts an array of events including car shows, music and live entertainment, historic tours, food vendors, and special children's activities.

The Red Carpet Corridor Festival includes thirteen communities along a ninety-mile section of Route 66 in northern Illinois. As with its counterpart, each community hosts an array of events that celebrate Route 66, as well as the towns' unique heritage and attributes. Towns included in this tour are Joliet, Elwood, Wilmington, Braidwood, Godley, Braceville, Gardner, Dwight, Odell, Pontiac, Chenoa, Lexington, and Towanda.

www.illinoisroute66.org

MERAMEC CAVERNS

Stunning scenic wonders, above and below ground, may be the main attractions at Meramec Caverns, but this resort complex is linked with legend, tall tales, history, a marketing genius, and, of course, Route 66.

In 1720, Philippe Renault of France was the first European explorer to see the caverns. Heavily laced with deposits of potassium nitrate, or saltpeter, a primary ingredient in the manufacture of gunpowder, the entrance chamber of the caverns became a focal point of mining for more than 150 years. In 1864, Confederate troops destroyed a Union gunpowder manufacturing facility here. By the 1890s, the entrance chamber, which had expanded because of mining, became a focal point for area entertainment with construction of a dance floor.

Acquisition of the property in 1933 by Lester Dill, a promoter worthy of P. T. Barnum, led to the transformation of the caverns into a major tourist attraction. In addition to marketing the scenic wonders, he built on local legend to link the caverns to Jesse James. Today, the caverns remain a primary attraction for Route 66 enthusiasts as well as travelers in southern Missouri.

1135 Hwy. W, Sullivan, MO 63080

www.americascave.com

RIALTO SQUARE THEATRE

From the stunning facade with its restored marquee and towering neon sign to the marble-walled rotunda lit by a stunning Duchess crystal chandelier, the Rialto Square Theatre is a true gem. Opened on May 24, 1926, the fully restored theater, consistently rated by historical architects as one of the most beautiful theaters in America, features a hundred hand-cut crystal chandeliers, extensive use of marble, and an array of colorful frescoes.

The original architects designed the inner lobby to mimic the Hall of Mirrors in the Palace of Versailles. The arch between the rotunda and esplanade, carefully modeled after the Arc de Triomphe in Paris, and the stunning blending of classic Greek, Roman, Byzantine, and Baroque elements continue the grand theme, making this a true movie palace.

102 N. Chicago St., Joliet, IL 60432

www.rialtosquare.com

TIP

If obscure historic sites are something you enjoy photographing, I suggest a stop in Wilmington, Illinois. Located at 100 Water Street is a rather nondescript two-story brick building. This is the oldest commercial structure along the Route 66 corridor in Illinois. Dating to about 1837, the Eagle Hotel established by David Lizer served as an inn and stage station. Over the years, it has housed a bank, a store, apartments, and a museum.

RED OAK II

Red Oak II is the creation of talented folk artist and visionary romantic Lowell Davis, who said, "I don't believe that an artist should be restricted to use only paint or clay. It can be anything including junk, wood, even an old building. To me, Red Oak II is a combination of a painting and a sculpture, and it is just made from things that someone else threw away."

Essentially, Red Oak II is a recreated Ozark Mountains farming community circa 1930s, built from historic buildings moved to the site and recreations of buildings. It's also a giant canvas for an array of diverse folk art creations. This gives the picturesque village a whimsical feel, a place where history and dreams flow together seamlessly. Visitors roam freely, explore the time-capsule buildings like the fully stocked general store, and discover wonderful folk art creations in the trees, in the streams, and throughout the grounds.

County Loop 122, Carthage, MO 64836

www.redoakiimissouri.com

COLEMAN THEATRE

Mining magnate George L. Coleman Sr. built the Coleman Theatre for a cost of $590,000 in 1929. Promoted as the most elaborate theater between Dallas and Kansas City when built, the structure is an architectural treasure. The Spanish Revival–style exterior is heavily decorated with terra-cotta ornamentation, wrought iron, and red tile roofs on the towers. However, the interior decor and appointments make this theater truly special.

Restored to their original splendor, winding staircases flanked by gilded statues holding candelabra provide access to the mezzanine, balcony seats, and ballroom. The carved mahogany, gold leaf, stained glass windows, colorful frescoes, and imported Venetian chandeliers are worthy of a theater in cities such as New York or San Francisco, and so the Coleman Theatre is a rare discovery in a small, rural Oklahoma community.

103 N. Main St., Miami, OK 74354

www.colemantheatre.org

CUBA FEST

Held every year on the third weekend in October, Cuba Fest is a delightful, old-fashioned, small-town event. Vendors offer an array of handcrafted items. There's also a chili cook-off giving local chefs an opportunity to share their favorite recipes, as well as music, street dancers, special activities for children, wine-tasting tents hosted by local wineries, storytellers in costume that illustrate the town's rich history, apple butter cooking, and a city wide "trolley" tour of its world-famous murals.

Evening activities are also a part of the weekend's festivities. The historic Wagon Wheel Motel hosts an open house that often features locally produced wines and presentations by critically acclaimed Route 66 authors. Belmont Winery, a few miles east of town, hosts a concert in their pavilion, where guests enjoy gourmet pizzas and other in-house specialties.

Cuba, MO 65453

www.cubamomurals.com

A short loop drive from Cuba to St. James, Missouri, with a stop at Maramec Spring Park is well worth the time, especially during the fall when stunning colors frame the fifth-largest natural spring in the state of Missouri. An average of one hundred million gallons of water flows from the submerged cavern daily. The park contains 1,860 acres of forest and fields. The 200-acre public use area provides visitors with many amenities including a cafe, store, campgrounds and campsites, wildlife viewing, fish feeding, picnicking, and playgrounds. The Meramec River, a clear, calm Ozark stream, flows through the park providing excellent fishing. Additional photo ops include the cemetery from a thriving nineteenth-century community that centered on the iron works established in 1826 and the massive stone remnants of the iron works themselves.

ED GALLOWAY'S TOTEM POLE PARK

Totem Pole Park is a folk art masterpiece located a short distance south of Foyil, Oklahoma. Dominating the park is a ninety-foot totem pole built in 1948 by manual arts teacher Ed Galloway with six tons of steel and twenty-eight tons of cement, rocks, and sand. The thirty-foot base is a turtle, and adorning the totem pole are several hundred bas-relief images.

Whimsical toadstool picnic tables are also a part of the complex, as are smaller totem poles, animal-form concrete gateposts, and an ornate barbecue. Serving as the visitor center is the ornately decorated, eleven-sided fiddle house supported inside and out by twenty-five concrete totem poles. The building houses some of Galloway's handcrafted fiddles, furniture, and bas-relief portraits of presidents up to John F. Kennedy. Several of his handcrafted items were never recovered after a robbery in 1970.

21300 E. Hwy. 28A, Chelsea, OK 74016

www.nps.gov/nr/travel/route66/galloways_totem_pole_park_foyil.html

OKLAHOMA CZECH FESTIVAL

The largest Czechoslovakian cultural event in the world outside the Czech Republic takes place in the heart of the Oklahoma prairie on the first Saturday of October each year. In an interview, Marjorie Jezek, president of Oklahoma Czech Inc., said, "The Czech Festival is our way of preserving and sharing the old Czech customs along with providing a part of the traditional Czech foods, so dear to the people of Czech descent. These customs and food recipes have been handed down from generation to generation."

The kickoff for the event is one of the largest parades in the state, along Main Street, Route 66. The parade features displays created by local businesses and civic groups and floats with the Oklahoma Czech Royalty Pageant contestants. Other activities include the Czech Royalty Coronation Ball, polka music and dancing, a carnival and petting zoo, one of the largest craft shows in Oklahoma, and an array of booths offering traditional Czech foods.

Yukon, OK

www.czechfestivaloklahoma.com

SEABA STATION MOTORCYCLE MUSEUM

It's not easy to overlook Seaba Station, since it's the only business in Warwick, Oklahoma, and one of the few remaining buildings. Built in 1921, the distinctly designed brick building constructed by John and Alice Seaba appears unchanged from photos taken during the Great Depression. Initially it served as a filling station, but shortly after opening John transformed it into a machine shop. An unlikely photo op here is the ruins of the former restrooms, an odd blending of outhouse with indoor plumbing that includes an unusual antique toilet.

In October 2007, Gerald Tims and Jerry Ries acquired the building, and after refurbishment, opened Seaba Station Motorcycle Museum. The historic shop is a fitting backdrop for a diverse array of motorcycles, some built in the early part of the twentieth century, as well as a few with a celebrity association. The station owners also host numerous events, including a very popular swap meet for motorcycle parts and a motorcycle and car show.

336992 E. Hwy. 66 , Chandler, OK 74834 (community of Warwick)

www.seabastation.com

The Museum of Transportation in suburban St. Louis, Missouri, is another place that has an interesting connection with Route 66. Located in this almost overwhelming collection of boats, aircraft, automobiles, motorcycles, and trains is a remnant of the Coral Court Motel. The demolition of this stylish and uniquely designed motel sparked the rise of the grassroots preservationist movement on Route 66. On display is a section of the motel's facade and a fully recreated room built from salvaged materials including glass bricks, windows, and flooring, and even some original furnishings.

HOLBROOK
ROUTE 66 FESTIVAL

The weather isn't the only thing heating up in Holbrook, Arizona, in the first weeks of June. The city's Route 66 Festival grows in scope, size, and popularity every year. What initially began as a small-town community get-together to celebrate Route 66 is now an event that attracts spectators and participants from around the world.

The festival is unique in that it's a celebration of Route 66 as well as Holbrook's colorful Western history. That means there are activities at the nineteenth-century Navajo County Courthouse that now houses a fascinating museum, as well as a Gunslinger Car Show, vendors, Hopis and Navajos performing traditional dances, and live bands. However, what really sets this event apart from other Route 66 festivals is the Route 66 Relics Tour.

This bus tour provides access to a section of Route 66 and related sites within the Petrified Forest National Park and Painted Desert. These are off-limits to the public except during this festival or by special arrangement.

Holbrook, AZ

www.goholbrook.com

RICHARDSON'S TRADING COMPANY

Unlike many of the trading posts located along Route 66, this is not just a curio shop that caters to tourists. A one-family-owned business since 1913, Richardson's Trading Company is an actual working trading post, but it's also a museum filled with items, artifacts, and photographs acquired during a century of trading with area tribes. Some of the trading customers are third and fourth generation.

The rug room featuring the finest Navajo rugs in the world is a primary attraction. There are exquisite displays of silverwork, pottery, beadwork, leatherwork, and woodcarving from Zuni, Navajo, and Hopi artisans. Curiosities and oddities are also on display, including a stuffed albino buffalo, a historic trader's wagon, a giant turquoise nugget, and a room outfitted to show a nineteenth-century reservation trading post.

222 W. Hwy. 66, Gallup, NM 87301

SANDIA PEAK TRAMWAY

The 2.7-mile Sandia Peak Tramway transports visitors from the high desert of the Rio Grande River Valley to the observation deck of Sandia Peak at 10,378 feet. The trip itself is nothing short of spectacular, as the tramway suspends passengers over deep and colorful canyons, pine-forested rocky knolls, and stone spires. The view from the observation deck or restaurant is even more awe inspiring. On a clear day, an estimated 11,000 square miles of desert, mountains, the Rio Grande River Valley, and the Cibola National Forest are on view. There's also a stunning panoramic view of Albuquerque.

Deemed an engineering marvel at the time of its completion, the tramway was built by Bell Engineering, a Swiss company that began building tramways in 1888. It required two years of construction and sixty days of testing before the first passengers rode to the summit on May 7, 1966.

30 Tramway Rd. NE, Albuquerque, NM 87122

www.sandiapeak.com

ANGEL & VILMA'S ORIGINAL ROUTE 66 GIFT SHOP

If it were not for the daily throngs of tourists and tour buses parked at the curb almost every day of the year, this unassuming small store and barbershop could easily be overlooked, even though colorful, whimsical displays grace the front facade and sidewalk and a few timeworn trucks and cars line the street in front. This, however, is the cornerstone of the Route 66 renaissance, and its proprietor, Angel Delgadillo, is perhaps the most famous personality on the highway.

Born in Seligman, Delgadillo watched the community enter a period of precipitous decline with the completion of I-40, which bypassed the town. Tapping into the romanticism and history of Route 66, he launched an initiative that resulted in the creation of the Arizona Route 66 Association, the first of its kind, and recognition of Route 66 as a historic byway by the state of Arizona. From these humble beginnings, the Route 66 renaissance became an international phenomenon that continues to grow.

22265 Historic Rte. 66, Seligman, AZ 86337

www.route66giftshop.com

TIP

Traveling during the summer is ideal for enjoying a roadside picnic, the ultimate time-capsule dining experience on Route 66. Counted among our favorite places is the general store in Parks, Arizona. The current store dates to 1921. In addition to the general merchandise, there's a quaint little deli at the back of the store and a picnic table on the opposite side of the highway. At an elevation of seven thousand feet, you are assured cool temperatures even in the midst of summer.

GRAND CANYON CAVERNS

This quirky stop should be on any list of must-see Route 66 attractions. A bucket on a rope provided initial access to the caverns, which were discovered in 1927. Owners of the property at the time jokingly referred to this as "dope on a rope." In the 1930s, development to transform the property into a tourist destination commenced in earnest, and ladders, stairs, and swinging bridges utilizing building materials salvaged from the Hoover Dam project were built to facilitate ease of access to the caverns. Twenty years later, installation of an elevator and paved trails and ever-increasing traffic on Route 66 helped transform this into the second most popular attraction in the state of Arizona.

Today the caverns feature handicap-accessible tours, spelunking opportunities, "the world's quietest motel suite," a lunchroom, and a performance stage. Aboveground are riding stables, a refurbished motel, a gift shop, a restaurant, an award-winning RV park, a most unusual miniature golf course, and a disc golf course.

Mile Marker 115, State Hwy. 66 (Route 66), AZ

www.gccaverns.com

Seventy scenic miles north of Kingman, at the west end of the Grand Canyon, is Grand Canyon West Resort. The highlight of a visit to this resort is the glass-bottomed skywalk that provides unparalleled views of the canyon. There's also an excellent restaurant located on the canyon rim and a recreated Western village where trail and wagon rides are available. A few miles west of the resort is Grand Canyon Western Ranch. This historic ranch established by Tap Duncan in the late nineteenth century now offers the ultimate dude ranch experience.

GATHERING OF NATIONS POWWOW

The Gathering of Nations Powwow and Miss Indian World Pageant, held on the fourth weekend in April, transform the New Mexico State Fairgrounds into the largest Native American cultural event in the United States. In addition to dancers from more than five hundred tribes performing traditional ceremonies, there are concerts and an Indian Traders Market featuring artists, crafters, traders selling indigenous arts and crafts, and tribal foods. There's a wide array of competitions for participants, including traditional singers in two categories—northern and southern tribes—as well as drum groups, dance categories for seniors seventy years of age or older, and even activities for tots and teenagers.

The event is a unique opportunity to experience the rich and diverse Native American culture. In addition, it's a family event that will provide years of memories.

Albuquerque, NM

www.gatheringofnations.com

ZETTLER'S ROUTE 66 STORE

In 1930, Homer and Marie Zettler opened a bakery in the building that now houses Zettler's Route 66 Store. After World War II, business was expanded to include a full-service meat market and grocery. Vernon, the couple's oldest son, kept the business going until he and his wife, Marge, retired in 1983. New owners kept the business going for almost thirty more years.

A new chapter for the store commenced on April 1, 2016, when Kirk and Yvette Slack reopened it after fifteen months of repair and cleaning. Innovative marketing through a "Life on the Mother Road" series of interviews with visitors on a YouTube channel and friendly service quickly transformed the old store into a destination for enthusiasts. The always changing inventory that ranges from Native American handicrafts, souvenirs, vintage motorcycle and automobile parts, antiques, and curiosities ensures that no two visits are the same.

242 W. Lewis Avenue, Ash Fork, AZ 86320

ROUTE 66 FUN RUN

The Route 66 Fun Run is the oldest continuous annual festival celebrating this storied old highway. In 2017, for the thirtieth anniversary event, participants traveled from as far as New Zealand to take part in the festivities. The event is essentially a three-day block party on the longest remaining uninterrupted—and arguably the most scenic—portion of Route 66, running between Seligman and Topock, Arizona. The Promote Kingman initiative markets this as "160 Miles of Smiles."

Held on the first weekend of May, the festival features a variety of events that take place in each of the communities along this corridor and at Grand Canyon Caverns and Keepers of the Wild Nature Park. The centerpiece of the event takes place on Saturday. It starts with a parade of entrants in Seligman and a send-off by Angel Delgadillo, who is recognized as a founder of the Route 66 renaissance, followed by a cruise along Route 66 to Kingman. In Kingman, several blocks of Route 66 along Andy Devine Avenue close to allow for the display of participating vehicles, often more than eight hundred vintage and antique cars and trucks, as well as colorful hotrods. Live music, vendors, and an evening of entertainment foster a festive atmosphere.

Kingman, AZ 86401

www.azrt66.com

If you brought your mountain bike and hiking shoes, the site of historic Fort Beale on the northwest side of Kingman, Arizona is the gateway to miles of scenic trails. The highlight must be the Monolith Gardens loop. Established at a spring that provided an abundant supply of year-round water, the fort named for Lt. Edward Fitzgerald Beale was a vital strongpoint during the Hualapai Wars of the 1870s. It also served as an oasis for travelers on the Beale Wagon Road and the Mojave-Prescott Toll Road. The location also served as the first Hualapai Indian Reservation and the starting point for that tribe's trail of tears. A monument at the gate commemorates that event. Information and a map of the trail system are available at the Powerhouse Visitor Center in Kingman. When inquiring about directions, I suggest that you also ask about how to locate the Stockton Hill Wagon Road less than two miles north of Kingman. The wagon ruts worn into the stone in the shadow of towering buttes is an interesting photo opportunity.

PECOS NATIONAL HISTORIC PARK

Located on the pre-1937 alignment of Route 66 east of Santa Fe, Pecos National Historic Park, in the shadow of Glorieta Pass, is a scenic wonder as well as a repository of historic artifacts spanning almost a thousand years. The centerpieces of the park are the ruins of the picturesque pueblo that dates to about AD 1200 and the mission built by the Spanish in the late sixteenth century.

The Santa Fe Trail, a primary trade route utilized between 1858 and 1880, coursed through the park, and remnants of the Kozlowski Stage Stop and Tavern were incorporated into the Forked Lightning Ranch headquarters and trading post in 1925. Greer Garson Fogelson sold the ranch to the Conservation Fund, which donated it to the National Park Service in 1991. In addition, a scenic 2.35-mile Glorieta Battlefield Trail provides access to the site of a pivotal battle during the Civil War.

Pecos, NM 87552

www.nps.gov/peco/index.htm

ALBUQUERQUE INTERNATIONAL BALLOON FESTIVAL

The humble beginning of this monster event was a gathering of thirteen balloons in 1972. Now, with the number of entries often exceeding one thousand balloons, it's the largest event of its kind in the world. In addition, with an estimated 25 million still photographs taken during the event, it has earned the title of the world's most photographed event. What started in a mall parking lot now requires a dedicated site of more than 350 acres.

While the colorful balloons and stunning landscapes that serve as the background are the centerpieces of the event, the festival has grown to include a wide array of activities. Framed by a beautiful New Mexico sunrise are the dawn patrol show and a mass ascension of balloons, as well as an afterglow fireworks show. There's also a laser light show and displays of competition flying.

Albuquerque, NM

www.balloonfiesta.com

BROADWAY THEATER DISTRICT

The heart of the historic theater district in Los Angeles centers on the intersection of 7th Street and Broadway, the original western terminus of Route 66. With twelve ornate historic theaters built between 1910 and 1931 on a six-block corridor, this is the largest district of its kind in the United States.

In the 1980s, after decades of decline, preservation commenced and initiatives were launched to reinvigorate the district. Formed in 1987, the Los Angeles Conservancy initiated several innovative programs to utilize the theaters and subsequently generate public awareness of the historic treasures. The district consists of the Million Dollar Theatre (1918), Roxie Theatre (1932), Cameo Theatre (1910), Arcade Theatre (1910), Los Angeles Theatre (1931), Palace Theatre (1911), State Theatre (1921), Globe Theatre (1913), Tower Theatre (1927), Rialto Theatre (1917), Orpheum Theatre (1926), and United Artists Theatre (1927).

300–849 S. Broadway, Los Angeles, CA

The Olvera District of Los Angeles (Calle Olvera) stands in stark contrast to the bustling metropolis that surrounds it. That makes it an ideal place to relax. This is the oldest historical district in the city and a part of El Pueblo de Los Angeles Historic Monument. The majority of the Plaza District's oldest historic buildings and monuments are on Olvera Street, as well as some of the oldest Los Angeles monuments including the Avila Adobe built in 1818, the Pelanconi House built in 1857, and the Sepulveda House built in 1887. Often listed as one of the greatest streets in America, the pedestrian mall marketplace with craft shops, restaurants, and roving troubadours is a popular destination for tourists and locals alike.

HOLLYWOOD FOREVER CEMETERY

Historic landmark, unique cultural venue for classic cinema and concerts, a beautifully landscaped park with a view of the classic hillside Hollywood sign, and an association with the rich and famous of Hollywood in the 1920s and 1930s—that is the Hollywood Forever Cemetery. Established in 1899, the cemetery is the oldest one in Los Angeles. It's also the final resting place for some of the most famous celebrities in Hollywood history, including Douglas Fairbanks Sr., Mel Blanc, Charles Chaplin Jr., Iron Eyes Cody, Cecil B. DeMille, Nelson Eddy, and even Toto, the dog from *The Wizard of Oz.*

Among the many unique aspects of this cemetery is the LifeStories project—multimedia kiosks that transform graves into living memorials with photos and audio and video clips. This cemetery is an unforgettable experience as well as a one-of-a-kind photo opportunity, but you need to register at the office if you'll be photographing the monuments.

6000 Santa Monica Blvd., Los Angeles, CA 90038

www.hollywoodforever.com

TIP

After working up an appetite exploring the Hollywood Forever Cemetery, stop at Barney's Beanery for a bite to eat. Located at 8447 Santa Monica Boulevard in West Hollywood, California, this restaurant is one of the oldest in continuous operation in Los Angeles County. Established in 1927, it has a rather unique decor as well as delicious menu offerings.

ACTIVITIES
BY SEASON

SPRING

Every year, on the first weekend in May, the annual Route 66 Fun Run transforms the longest remaining uninterrupted segment of Route 66 into a 140-mile fun fest. From Seligman to Topock, Arizona, iconic Route 66 becomes a living time capsule as hundreds of classic cars, hot rods, vintage trucks, and even rental cars driven by enthusiasts from as far away as Canada fill the road, crowd the diners and restaurants, and pack parking lots at classic attractions such as Grand Canyon Caverns.

SUMMER

Summer is the ideal time for a very short detour and a bit of time travel. Only accessed from Route 66, Supai, where the mail is delivered by mule train, is the most remote community in America. To reach the village requires a scenic drive of sixty miles from the junction of Indian Highway 18 and Route 66, and then either an eight-mile hike into a deep canyon, an exhilarating helicopter ride, or a trip on a rented horse.

The village nestled within a deep canyon, home of the Havasupai people, is only the first stop on this adventure. A few miles further down the canyon is a series of stunning waterfalls that fall from red rock walls into turquoise lagoons and campgrounds. One of these is actually taller than Niagara Falls.

FALL

Wineries, roadside produce stands along gently twisting mountain roads, and stunning displays of fall color make the Missouri Ozarks the perfect place for a Route 66 adventure during the fall. To enhance your visit, add a traditional small-town fall harvest festival.

Cuba, Missouri, is ideally located for a Route 66 experience in the Ozarks. Cuba Fest on the third weekend in October is reminiscent of a Norman Rockwell print. 4M Farms produce store, located a few miles west of town along Route 66, is filled with regional and traditional favorites like sorghum, apple cider, fresh-baked cherry pie, and a variety of jellies. The stunning natural beauty of Meramec Springs State Park is just a few miles south of town, and Bob's Gasoline Alley with its vast collection of service station and oil company signs, equipment, and memorabilia is located less than five miles from town.

WINTER

The months of winter are the ideal time to explore the wonders of Route 66 in western Arizona and in the California desert. You can ski in Flagstaff, Arizona, and do a bit of sunbathing along the Colorado River all in the same day!

As you won't have to worry about snakes or 120-degree days, hikes and long walks will enhance the Route 66 adventure. The nineteenth-century Johnson Canyon railroad tunnel is accessed via an early alignment of Route 66 near Ash Fork, the historic Kelso railroad station is your portal to the Mojave National Preserve, and the trail to the summit of Amboy Crater is a scenic wonder. The Cerbat Foothills trail system near Kingman, Arizona, provides access to the site of Fort Beale and Monolith Gardens.

INDEX